INDIA'S APPROACH TO THE TIBETAN QUESTION AND ITS IMPACT ON SINO-INDIAN RELATIONS

Dr. B. K. TYAGI

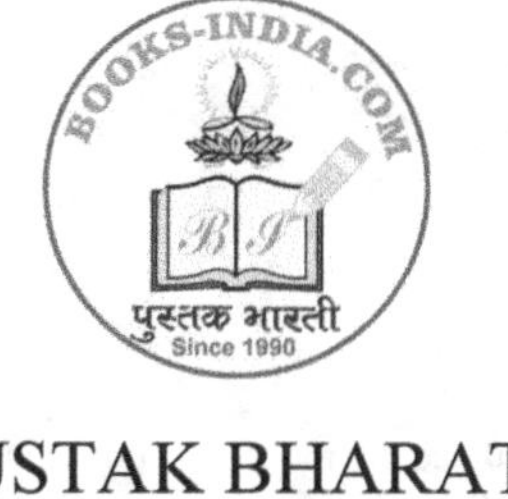

PUSTAK BHARATI
TORONTO, CANADA

Author: Dr. Bhuwneshwer Kumar Tyagi

Title: INDIA'S APPROACH TO THE TIBETAN QUESTION AND ITS IMPACT ON SINO-INDIAN RELATIONS

Publisher: Pustak Bharati, Toronto, Canada.

180 Torresdale Ave, Toronto Canada M2R 3E4

www.pustak-bharati-canada.com

pustak.bharati.canada@gmail.com

ISBN : 978-1-897416-22-8

ISBN 978-1-897416-22-8
90000

9 781897 416228

Copyright ©2019

To My Parents,

who are in their Heavenly abode, and whose blessings are ever
with me.

ABBREVIATIONS

ATPD- Assembly of Tibetan People's Deputies

BRI- Belt and Road Initiative

CPEC- China Pakistan Economic Corridor

CPI- Communist Party of India

CTA- Central Tibetan Administration

ICESCR- International Covenant on Economic, Social and Cultural Rights

NCNA- National Communist News Agency

NEF- North East Frontier Agency

OBOR- One Belt One Road

PLA- People's Liberation Army

PRC- People's Republic of China

TAR- Tibet Autonomous Region

TYC- Tibetan Youth Congress

USCIRF- United States Commission on International Religious Freedom

CONTENTS

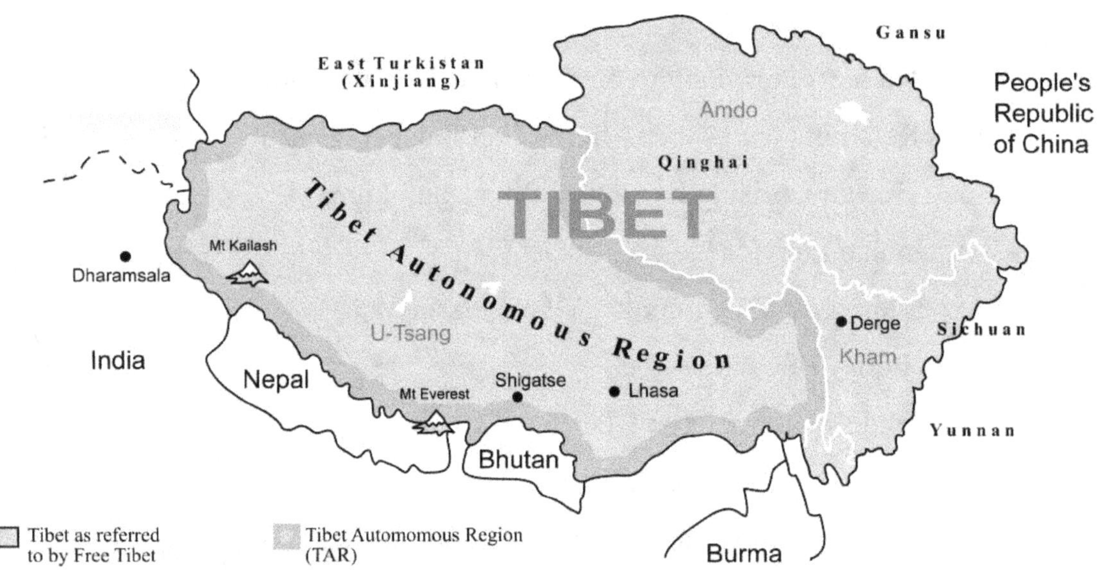

Geographical Situation of Tibet

PREFACE

The present work is a study of the Tibetan Question and Its Impact on Sino-Indian Policies. Relation of India with Tibet has been culturally, economically, religiously, and politically very strong since times immemorial. These relations were obstructed by various political factors; yet at the end they can be said to have continued during the colonial period of the supremacy of British Government on Indian subcontinent.

Historically Tibet has served as a buffer zone between India and China. In 1959, China occupied Tibet and since then the border has became a contentious issue between India and China. The Indian Prime Minister Jawaharlal Nehru made substantial efforts to create peace with China and they reached an agreement, which is known as the *Panchsheela* agreement. This was Nehru's strategy to build a partnership with China to consolidate the non-alignment movement in the world.

The purpose of this piece of research is to analyze the relations of these two regions for establishment of new milestones of friendship which will be fruitful for the progressing India and the State of Tibet, with their modern resources.

Political experts in India have been openly critical of China's handling of Tibetans' quest for autonomous rule and their desire to preserve an independent culture, while being pragmatic about the need to forge good relations with China.

Since the Dalai Lama first fled China in 1959 to India after a failed Tibetan uprising, India has maintained a nuanced position. The Indian government, while sympathetic to the case of the Dalai Lama, contends that Tibet legally is a part of China.

The study is primarily based on the records and material available in Library of Tibetan Works and Archives, Dharamsala, records published by the Secretary, Department of Information and International Relations, Central Tibetan Administration

Gangchen Kyishong, Dharmshala. The travelogues of The British, Indian and Chinese travellers were consulted, who visited Tibet and narrated their valuable information in their works. The contemporary unpublished and published works of different scholars from Asia and Europe were also consulted. Regarding the Indo-Tibetan and Sino-Indian activities books and articles in different Journals and e-books available on different websites functioned as resources.

I am gratefully acknowledge the cooperation received from the staff of the Library of Tibetan Works and Archives, Dharamsala, Department of Information and International Relations, Central Tibetan Administration Gangchen Kyishong, Dharmshala, Director and staff Library ICHR, New Delhi, Central Secretariat Library, New Delhi where I consulted in detail the source material for my research.

I feel obliged to my friend and senior scholar Dr.J.K.Nair, Professor of English, J.N.S. Government (P.G.) College, Shujalpur (Shajapur) for his valuable and technical suggestions and help during the course of my research. I am also thankful to my friend Dr. Brijesh Pare Professor of Chemistry and Mr. D. K. Budholiya, Assistant Professor (English) for their valuable suggestions. I am thankful to Dr Rakesh Kumar Dubey, my friend and secretary Pustak Bharti Toronto for helping and publishing this book under his valuable guidance. I am also oblised to Pustak Bharti Toronto for publishing this book.

Last but not the least; I am deeply grateful to my wife Dr. Archana Tyagi, my daughter Miss Vishakha Tyagi, a creative art director DDB Mudra for designing cover page, graphics and other valuable suggestions and my son Shantanu Tyagi an aspirant of sports, leisure and tourism management for his valuable suggestions. Without their cooperation and encouragement this study would not have been possible.

Dr. Bhuwnesher Kumar Tyagi

INTRODUCTION

Relation of India with Tibet has been culturally, economically, religiously, and politically very strong since times immemorial. These relations were obstructed by various political factors; yet at the bottom they can be said to have continued during the colonial period of the supremacy of British Government on Indian subcontinent. Two factors make Tibet important for India in today's context (a) the religious and cultural factors; (b) ecological factors. It argues that Tibet with Tibetan Buddhists provides better security than a Hanised Tibet.

Tibet known as the 'roof of the world' is an Asian nation, situated between the two ancient civilizations of China and India, separated from the former by the mountain ranges to the east of the Tibetan Plateau and from the latter by the towering Himalayas. Through all the ages Tibet has held a paramount position amongst those regions of the world which have been popularly invested with a veil of mystery because they are unreachable and unknown.

Tibet geographically is a high plateau in the centre of Asia. It lies roughly within the 28th and 36th parallels of north latitude and 79th and 99th of east longitude and has common frontiers with both China and India. It marches with China for approximately 1400 miles along the borders of Yunnan, Szechuan, and Kansu provinces and 1300 miles more with Sinkiang. With the Indian states of Sikkim and Kashmir and with Bhutan and Nepal it has some 2000 miles of common borders. The frontiers of Russia do not touch Tibet at any point. Chinese Turkestan separates the two countries. History and tradition show that Tibet lies within the scope of Russian expansion in Central Asia. Hence her geographical position has made her the political junction of Asia's three largest land powers, China, India and Russia. Consequently she has played a significant role in the development of Sino-Indian relations.

It is striking to note that from the seventh to the ninth centuries the Tibetans were able to keep up their widespread military activity under the long line of the Gampo Kings. Bell writes[1] that neither China nor India escaped invasion by the Tibetans. This period was characterised by relations on a footing of equality and reciprocity between Tibet, China, and India.

Tibet was independent till almost the 12th century A.D. In 1200 when the Mongols launched their world conquests from the Altai Karakorum the Tibetan chiefs brought peace with Chenghiz Khan by an offer of submission in 1207. His grandson Kublai Khan recognised the political advantages of a religious link with Tibet and became a convert to Lamaism in 1270.[2]

Geographical Features:

So unique is the position of Tibet that a short description of its physical characteristics is almost essential to a comprehension of successive methods of exploration. Modern Indian geologists are disposed to associate the upheaval of Tibet with that of the great trans-Indus table-lands of Baluchistan and Afghanistan on the west, with the north-western Himalayas on the south, and the northern Burmese mountains on the east; that is to say, they consider it to be very much more recent than the central portions of the Indian peninsula, or of the Himalayas to the northeast

---

[1] Charles Bell, A Unique Figure in World History, 'Portrait of the Dalai Lama' p. 210. There were 32 legendary kings before him.
[2] L.A. Waddell, Lhasa and its Mysteries, London, 1905, p. 26.

of India. This contention appears to be justified by the discovery of certain forms of fossils indicating the existence of life which has nowhere been found in the great highland steppes of the Asiatic continent, or in the broad expanse of the ancient beds of Central India. When man made his first appearance is not a matter of discussion, but there can be no reasonable doubt that the Tibetan is the latest survival of the ancient Turko-Mongol stock which once prevailed through all high Asia. The Tibetans came from the northeast in a purely Mongol form, and later from the southeast, from Burma and Assam in the form of the Tibeto-Burman of modern ethnology, who aforetime occupied a great part of northern India.

The valley of the *Brahmaputra*, of the Subansiri, and of those eastern affluent of the *Brahmaputra* which are separated from the sources of the *Irawadi* only by the narrow Patkoi range, were once the main avenues of approach to Tibet. It is worth noting that the Tibetan himself claims descent from the monkey.

Within the limits of the recognised Tibetan frontier we have three great physical divisions of vastly elevated plain which it is important to distinguish from each other.

First, the great northern plateau flanked by the Kuen Lun and the steppe of Tsaidam, which is known as the Chang tang. This is the region of highest elevation, too high and too cold for anything but pastoral use, where salt lakes are scattered at intervals amidst vast sterile flats, where grass is scanty and trees are absolutely wanting. It is sparsely inhabited by Mongolian nomads. Intensely cold, wind-swept, storm-beaten, and barren, it is perhaps the most inhospitable region in Asiatic world. The Chang is the true Tibetan bulwark of the Indian frontier. It is impossible for large bodies of people, and has proved to be almost impassable for small companies.

Second, the upper valley of the Indus and Brahmaputra and their affluent, some of which are large rivers, e.g., the Kyichu, on which stands Lhasa. At the parting of waters where the Indus, the Sutlej, and the Brahmaputra divide to the west and east, southern Tibet is high; but for three hundred miles to the northwest, and for seven hundred miles to the southeast and east, the level gradually diminishes to about thirteen thousand feet near the Ladakh frontier, and eleven thousand feet on the Brahmaputra, south of Lhasa. The upper Indus contains some notable towns, which are local centres of trade, such as Gartok, Demchok, etc., and is not devoid of the softer beauty of lower Himalayan scenery beneath the stupendous cliffs and crags of the ranges stretching north of Kailas. Although there is no town in Tibet that would rank as second class in India, there are imposing collections of stone-built, white – faced houses dominated by ever-prevalent monastic buildings, which are quite equal in the scale of township with the secondary towns of Afghanistan or Baluchistan; and indeed are not unlike the townlets that may be seen clinging to the spurs of the Hindu Kush north of Kabul. Tadum, Janglache, and Shigatze are the most important towns west of Lhasa.

Third, the eastern mountains and valleys desolate steppes of Tsaidam on the northeast to the rim of the Brahmaputra basin north of Lhasa, the eastern edge of the great central Chang Tang forms an orographical feature which is of vast importance in the physical conformation of eastern Asia. Here arise innumerable rivulets which gather their infant forces together to form the first affluent of the great rivers of china, of Siam (Thailand), and of Burma.

The chief obstacles to Tibetan exploration have ever been the mountain barriers which surround the plateau, rather than the plateau itself. These mountain systems on all sides of Tibet are massed into a series of gigantic walls, the ranges and ridges of which are not fashioned as long spurs reaching out from the highlands and gradually diminishing in altitude till they fade into the plains below, enclosing long sloping valleys which would answer the purpose of ramps or shelving approaches to the heights; but they are folded range after range in gigantic altitudes, forming a rough but readily recognisable system of parallel flexure flanking the general edge of the central Tibetan upheaval.

Tibet may be described as a huge pear-shaped formation, with the small end of the pear attached to the south-eastern corner of the Pamirs at the point where the Kashmir hinterland, from the heights of the giant Muztagh range, looks northward over the sources of the rivers of Chinese Turkestan or eastern Turkestan. The Muztagh range might almost be called the stem of the pear, the narrow end of the pear gradually widening out therefrom being appropriately known as Little Tibet. Little Tibet is politically an outlying province of Kashmir. As the northern side of the pear-shaped formation curves boldly eastward it is represented by the border mountain systems of Kuen Lun, Altyn Tagh, Nan Shan etc., which, following each other in succession, carry the northern boundary of Tibet to the province of Kansu of China. Where exactly Kansu ends and Tibet begins is a matter rather of conjecture than political certainty. Throughout the Kuen Lun series of mountain systems there is a certain structural similarity. The main ranges are folded in vast anticlinals parallel to the edge of Tibet and to one another, ridge like a series of walls.

On the east, at the broad end of the pear-shaped plateau, the mountains of the Kansu border curve round southward and gradually merge into a fairly well-defined north to south range which figures on the map as Sifan. Here, within the limits of

Tibet, there occurs the commencement of a most remarkable orographical feature. Range after range striking outwards from the plateau follows the same curving course from southeast to south, bending in orderly procession like the waves of the sea, deepening their valleys and steepening their sides as they proceed southwards, till the whole south-eastern world of Tibet is but a succession of mountain waves whose forest-crested summits gradually reach southwards into Burma. Down the deep troughs of these south-eastern valleys of Tibet flow the waters of several of the most important rivers of Asia. The Dichu or Yang-tse is the outermost, with a course of eight hundred miles before it passes the Tibetan frontier. The Mekong, the river of Burma, flows within the Yang-tse, and parallel to it. Recent evidence points to the fact that the Irawadi, the next great Burmese river, does not rise far, if at all, within the Tibetan border.

The structural relationship of the Himalayan ranges on the south of Tibet is very similar to that of the mountains on the north. Throughout their whole length, from the great bend of the Indus to the Brahmaputra through fifteen hundred miles of mountains, there runs a dominant water-parking or backbone to the whole system. This is set back from the plains of India at a distance of about one hundred miles. It is on this divide that the magnificent array of highest snow-capped peaks is to be found, from the giants of Kashmir to the groups of pinnacle about Everest and Kanchenjunga.

According to the writings of early Tibetan scholars[3], the name 'Bod' or Tibet had originated from the name 'Pugyal' long before the Bon religion emerged. Others maintain that the name 'Bod' was derived from Bon itself, which is the name of the

---

[3] Deb Bahadur Thapa, Tibet Past and Present, History, Culture and Society, Vol. I, p. 1.

early religion of the country before the introduction of Buddhism. Yet another group of scholars maintain that the name Bod, orally meaning 'fled' was given to the country because the Indian leader Rupati and his followers fled to Tibet after involvement in war with the Pandavas, it is also stated that 'Bod" has no specific meaning and it is used merely as a form of identification. The Indo-Tibetan border residents refer to Tibetans as Botias, a name derived from 'Bhota' the Sanskrit name for Tibet.

The modern name of Tibet by which the country is known to the world derives from the Mongolian 'Thubet', the Chinese 'Tufan' the Thai 'Thibet' and the Arabic 'Tubbat' which are found in early works of scholars. In the many poetical writings of Tibet, the country is referred to as 'Khawachen' or 'Gangjong' meaning 'The Abode of Snow' and Sildanjong meaning 'the Cool climate land'.

There was a stone pillar, the Lhasa Zhol *rdo-rings*, in the ancient village of Zhol in front of the Potala in Lhasa, dating to c. 764 CE during the reign of Trisong Detsen. It also contains an account of the brief capture of Chang'an, the Chinese capital, in 763 CE during the reign of Emperor Daizong of Tang. As of 1993 the pillar was surrounded by buildings and wire so it could not be approached closely.

In 785, Wei Kao, a Chinese serving as an official in Shuh repulsed Tibetan invasions of the area. A stone monument dating to 823 and setting out the terms of peace and also determining the borders between Tibet and China, arrived at in 821, can still be seen in front of the Jokhang temple in Barkhor Square in Lhasa. The monument, a treaty of friendship, is written in both Tibetan and Chinese. The inscribed pillar was erected by the Chinese in 1793 during a smallpox epidemic. It records the Sino-Tibetan treaty of 822 concluded by King Ralpacan and includes the following inscription: "Tibet and China shall abide by the frontiers of which they are now in occupation. All to the east is the country of Great China; and all to the west is, without question, the country of Great Tibet. Henceforth on neither side shall there be waging of war nor seizing of territory. If any person incurs suspicion he shall be arrested; his business shall be inquired into and he shall be escorted back." The inscription also carried advice on hygiene measures to prevent smallpox.

The relations between the two countries appear to have been complex. On the one hand, the monument describes connections between China and Tibet as similar to those between uncle and nephew. The Tang dynasty of China and the Yarlung dynasty of Tibet were indeed related by marriage, yet the terms uncle and nephew are not used in relation to other groups with whom the Chinese had connections by marriage. On the other hand, the monument seems to describe the two countries as equals.

Conquest of Mongol:

Tibet has a history dating back to over 2,000 years. A good starting point in analysing the country's status is the period referred to as Tibet's "imperial age", when the entire country was first united under one ruler. There was no serious dispute over the existence of Tibet as an independent state during this period. Even China's own historical records and the treaties Tibet and China concluded during that period refer to Tibet as a strong state with whom China was forced to deal on an equal footing. International law protects the independence of Nation States from attempts to destroy them and, therefore, the presumption is in favour of the continuation of the statehood.

This means that whereas an independent state such as Tibet that has existed for centuries, does not need to prove its continued independence when challenged, a foreign state claiming sovereign rights over it needs to prove those rights by showing at what precise moment and by what legal means they were acquired.

Tibet continued to be an independent country outside the pale of the Manchu Empire until the first quarter of the eighteenth century. In 1728 the suppression of a civil war in Tibet was followed by the stationing of a Chinese expeditionary force at Lhasa, in aid of the Dalai Lama's Government.[4]

During the Manchu rule, influence over Tibet was never based on the willing consent of the rulers and the ruled of Tibet. Manchu supervision of Tibet through the Ambans was neither rigid nor regular. In 1750 when Ghurme Namgya organized an anti-Chinese rising he was decoyed at the hands of the Ambans, who killed him and they in turn were murdered by a Tibetan mob.[5]

China's present claim to Tibet is based entirely on the influence the Mongol and Manchu emperors exercised over Tibet in the 13th and 18th centuries, respectively. To claim that Tibet became a part of China because both countries were independently subjected to varying degrees of Mongol control, as the People's Republic of China does, is absurd.

This relatively brief period of foreign domination over Tibet occurred 700 years ago. Tibet broke away from the Yuan emperor before China regained its independence from the Mongols with the establishment of the native Ming Dynasty.

---

[4] L. Petech, China and Tibet in the early 18th Century, Leiden, 1950, p.108-124.
[5] L. Petech, op. cit., pp.199-216.

Not until the 18th century did Tibet once again come under a degree of foreign influence.

The Ming Dynasty, which ruled China from 1368 to 1644, had few ties with and no authority over Tibet. On the other hand, the Manchus, who conquered China and established the Qing Dynasty in the 17th century, embraced Tibetan Buddhism as the Mongols had and developed close ties with the Tibetans.

Chinese influence in Tibet between 1720 and 1912 ebbed and flowed with the changing fortunes of Manchu dynasty in China proper, and what is more interesting is the fact that the Chinese Ambans were able to exert some amount of influence in Tibet only during the minority of the Dalai Lamas or during the interregnum periods between the two Dalai Lamas.

At the political level, some powerful Manchu emperors succeeded in exerting a degree of influence over Tibet but they did not incorporate Tibet into their empire, much less China. Manchu influence did not last for very long. It was entirely ineffective by the time the British briefly invaded Tibet in 1904.

From 1911 to 1950, Tibet successfully avoided undue foreign influence and behaved, in every respect, as a fully independent state. The 13th Dalai Lama emphasised his country's independent status externally, in formal communications to foreign rulers, and internally, by issuing a proclamation reaffirming Tibet's independence and by strengthening the country's defences.

Tibet remained neutral during the Second World War, despite strong pressure from China and its allies, Britain and the USA. The Tibetan Government maintained independent international relations with all neighbouring countries, most of whom had diplomatic representatives in Lhasa.

The attitude of most foreign governments with whom Tibet maintained relations implied their recognition of Tibet's independent status. The British Government bound itself not to recognise Chinese sovereignty or any other rights over Tibet until and unless China signed the draft Shimla Convention of 1914 with Britain and Tibet, which China never did.

The turning point in Tibet's history came in 1949, when the People's Liberation Army of the PRC first crossed into Tibet. After defeating the small Tibetan army, the Chinese Government imposed on the Tibetan Government the so-called "Seventeen-Point Agreement for the Peaceful Liberation of Tibet" in May 1951.

Since it was signed under duress, the agreement was void under international law. The presence of 40,000 troops in Tibet, the threat of an immediate occupation of Lhasa and the prospect of the total obliteration of the Tibetan state left Tibetans with little choice. From a legal standpoint, Tibet has to this day not lost its statehood. It is an independent state under illegal occupation.

The Dalai Lama Rises to Power:

The Potala Palace in Lhasa was constructed as a symbol of this new synthesis of power. The Dalai Lama made a state visit to the Qing Dynasty's second Emperor, Shunzhi, in 1653. Each man bestowed honours and titles upon the other, and the Dalai Lama was recognized as the spiritual authority of the Qing Empire.

According to Tibet, the "priest/patron" relationship established at this time between the Dalai Lama and Qing China continued throughout the Qing Era, but it had no bearing on Tibet's status as an independent nation. China, naturally, disagrees.

Lobsang Gyatso died in 1682, but his Prime Minister concealed the Dalai Lama's death until 1696 so that the Potala Palace could be finished and the power of the Dalai Lama's office consolidated.

A look at the history of Tibet too would reveal that China invaded Tibet and has virtually converted it into its colony. Since the Chinese Revolution of 1911, when the Chinese forces were withdrawn from Tibet, Tibet had enjoyed de facto independence and had opposed Chinese attempts to reassert control. Even prior to 1911, Tibet had only acknowledged suzerainty (and not sovereignty) of the Manchu Emperors and their control fluctuated between military presence to a nominal link. It is interesting to note that in history there were periods when China was under the suzerainty of the Tibetan Emperor. The Tibetan Emperor Trisong Detsan (755-797 A.D.) invaded parts of China including Chengan (now Xian) and forced China to pay tribute to Tibet and accept Tibetan suzerainty. In 1821 a treaty between Tibet and China was concluded which agreed upon the fact that both the nations were independent.

The British, noting the situation, had always been treating Tibet as an autonomous region under the nominal Chinese suzerainty. British made several attempts after 1911 to bring China and Tibet together to accept this situation but the attempts always broke down on the issue of boundary between China and Tibet and not between Tibet and India. Eventually, the British presented the Chinese government in 1921 with a declaration to the effect that they did not feel justified in withholding any longer their recognition of the status of Tibet as an autonomous state under the suzerainty of China, and that they intended dealing on that basis with Tibet in the future. The British, after 1921, promised support to the Tibetan government in maintaining the latter's practical autonomy which was considered important to the security of India and to the tranquillity of India's north-eastern frontier. The above policy was clearly laid down in the memorandum issued by the British government on 23rd June 1943. The British PM Antony Eden on November 5, 1945 reiterated this in writing to the Chinese foreign minister Dr T. V. Soong.

After 1947, the Indian authorities too continued with this policy. When China invaded Tibet in 1950, Sardar Patel the then Deputy PM of India, in a note to the then secretary general in the external affairs ministry, Sir Girja Shankar Bajpai detailing the implications of the Chinese moves in Tibet, stated that the Chinese invasion had completely changed the security calculations and clearly pointed out that a serious danger was developing in the north and north east. He also agreed with the latter that 'a reconsideration of our military position and a redisposition of our forces were inescapable.' Sardar Patel later sent this note to the then Indian PM J L Nehru outlining the need for taking suitable action for India's defence. He clearly spelt out the strategic implications in the following lines-

"We have also to take note of a thoroughly unscrupulous, unreliable and determined power practically at our doors. The invasion of Tibet in my judgment, entitles us to treat them with a certain amount of hostility, let alone a great deal of circumspection. In these circumstances, one thing, to my mind, is quite clear; and, that is, that we cannot be friendly with China and must think in terms of defence against a determined, calculating, unscrupulous, ruthless, and unprincipled and prejudiced combination of powers, of which the Chinese will be the spearhead."

He certainly had Pakistan in mind when he talked of combination of powers. In the detailed note to Bajpai, he had mentioned that the threat from the West and North West had not reduced. How accurate his assessment was can be seen in the present context.

Unfortunately India's policy of non-interference allowed the Chinese government to impose 17-Point Agreement on Tibet under compulsion. The immediate consequence of this was that the Indo-Tibetan border became Sino-Indian border – a situation the British had tried to avoid at all costs. The trade agreement signed in 1954 was based on *Panchsheela* principles and that in effect buried the de facto independent Tibet nation. After this, India in the hope of managing China, signed a number of agreements that showed that India had accepted Tibet as an autonomous region of China. These included Agreement on Maintenance of Peace and Tranquillity along the Line of Actual Control in the India-China Border of 1993, Agreement between China and India on the Confidence Building Measures in the Military Field along the Line of Actual Control in the India- China Border Areas of 1996, Declaration on Principles for Relations and Comprehensive Cooperation of People's Republic of China and Republic of India of 2003 and Agreement between the Government of Republic of India and the Government of the People's Republic of China on Political Parameters and Guiding Principles for the Settlement of India-China Boundary Question of 2005. The text of these high sounding agreements would reflect that both sides would not do anything that would increase tension on the border and that both sides are sincere in resolving the issue through peaceful means. However, the Chinese actions have been contrary to the contents of these agreements.

In addition to the lack of sincerity on the part of the Chinese in making these agreements, they could not be implemented as there was no agreement on the length of the Sino-Indian border. While China does not include the area of J&K and considers Arunachal Pradesh as part of Tibet, India considers the entire length of the border between Tibet and India as Sino-Indian border. With this ambiguity, there are bound to be problems in the resolution of the issue. However, these agreements placed India in a disadvantageous position. India in these agreements accepted the Tibetan Autonomous Region as a part of China without obtaining any commitment from China on the issue of Jammu & Kashmir or Arunachal Pradesh. Even after the 2003 agreement, which agreed to the establishment of a trading mart in Nathula in Sikkim, Chinese maps continued to show Sikkim as an independent nation. Whenever, this issue was raised, the Chinese authorities brushed it aside by saying that they had inherited this from history and there was no need to give importance to the issue.

However, the basic issue is not what China is projecting through various statements and agreements but it is the intention of China towards India, which needs to be analysed in the light of its activities. Several experts have pointed out that China has encircled India by developing its strategic relations in our neighbourhood and desires to keep India under pressure so that it may not emerge as a strong nation. The Chinese activities certainly reveal this intention. China in the name of "Four Modernization" focussed on developing its armed forces and building infrastructure along the border. The recent aggressiveness shown in all the bordering areas reflects the intents of grabbing all the disputed areas along the Chinese borders. Its continued assistance in nuclear and missile fields to Pakistan is certainly affecting India's security and this cannot be regarded as a friendly act.

CHAPTER I

INDIA'S RELATION WITH TIBET:
A HISTORICAL PERSPECTIVE

Tibet with an area of 2.5 million sq. km. and with an average altitude of over 4,000 meters is pertinently known as the roof of the world. Because of its distinctive geographical features Tibet has produced a unique culture and way of life. According to their[6] needs and climatic conditions the Tibetans have acquired clothing habits from Mongolia, certain eating habits from China, and adopted the medical sciences of Iran and Afghanistan. Most important of all, the Buddhism and various traditions of arts and sciences came from India and deeply influenced the growth of Tibet's unique civilization. This is evident from the constant references made by Tibetan scholars to Indian scholarship and even to the mentioning of famous mountains and rivers of India in their literature.[7]

Tibet as a neighbour provided security for India's long northern border and because of its special geographic features became a safe haven for the preservation of Indian culture during the major upheavals on the subcontinent. As a nation Tibet practiced the Buddhist tenets of non-violence and peaceful existence. Tibet did not indulge in acts of aggression and, until this situation changed recently, Tibet served as an ideal buffer State between India and China.

---

[6] Dalai Lama, Memorandum from His Holiness the Dalia Lama to Prime Minister of India, Thenchen Choeling, Dharmsala Cantt. Kangra District Himachal Pradesh, May 29, 1985, p. 20.

[7] Ibid p. 21.

Tibetan culture is inseparably linked to Tibetan Buddhism. Over the last 1,000 years, Tibet has developed a unique, spiritual and peaceful culture with Buddhism at its heart. Many people's lives are dedicated to Tibetan Buddhism, which features elaborate rituals and advanced philosophical discussion.

The belief in reincarnation and the role of Lamas are also fundamental aspects of this school of Buddhism. The faith grew when an influx of Central Asian Buddhists flooded Tibet early in the eighth century, fleeing from advancing armies of Arab and Kazakh Muslims.

Recent changes, however, have pushed the Tibetans, who are by nature calm, gentle and kind, into an atmosphere of suspicion, fear and terror. Suicides almost unheard of in the past are common today. The Tibetan culture, which has developed over the centuries, has been destroyed completely and Tibet has been turned into a military base.[8] As a result six million Tibetans have lost their peace and their fundamental human rights, and these developments in Tibet now posed a new threat to its neighbouring countries, especially to India, which previously did not require a single armed person at her northern borders. Huge numbers of troops are stationed throughout the year in uninhabitable, difficult terrain high in the Himalayas. These new circumstances have caused an unnecessary financial burden for India, and disturbed the peace of Asia and the world at large. The relationship between Tibet and China is not a recent happening, it spans a period of over thirteen centuries during which there have been times when these two nations lived as friendly neighbours and also times when they fought one another when the Communist China forcefully occupied Tibet.

---

[8] Dalai Lama, Memorandum from His Holiness, p. 21.

Initially Tibetan view on the issue of Chinese invasion and occupation of Tibet was purely political and military and there was no strong evidence of racial confrontation or racial enmity against the Chinese in the minds of Tibetans. But in later period and presently in Tibet the Chinese are always seen in a negative light by the Tibetans and vice versa[9]. The Tibetans have now developed a strong racial enmity towards the Chinese.

The Chinese, on the other hand, because of their past experiences, are now compelled to explore new ideas and widen their relations with the outside world. In the process, they are becoming more responsive to world opinion which they cannot afford to ignore,. As for the Tibetans, unlike in the early sixties, there is now, widespread interest in Indian religion and culture. There is a growing number of Indians who are becoming aware of and sympathetic to the Tibetan people.

The British should have some sort of contact with Tibet was inevitable. The influence of Tibet extended far beyond its political frontiers. All along the Himalayas, in Ladakh, Lahul, Spiti, Garhwal, Kumaon, Nepal, Sikkim, Bhutan and Assam, as Burma and Western China from Yunnan to Kansu, were found people with close ties of race and religion to Tibet. Many states outside the normally accepted political frontiers of Tibet owed political allegiance to Ladakh were intimately involved with commercial relations. Trade across the Himalayas and trade between China and Tibet was a expression of politics as well as of economics. Trade was also connected with religion, in that many of Tibetan monasteries were involved in trade, and many goods coming to and from the markets of Tibet were carried by pilgrims. Political changes, therefore, on either side of the Tibetan frontier had

---

[9] Ibid p. 22.

commercial consequences; and attempts to alter the traditional patterns of trade had political effects.

While Indo-Tibetan trade has never been a vital element in the commerce of the Indian subcontinent, it has always been of great importance to the economic life of the Himalayan states; and, in consequence, any change in its volume or direction has had an effect on the political stability of India's northern frontier. To the East India Company, when its territory first began to extend towards the Himalayas, this trade had an added importance in that in the 18th century and Tibet bought more from India than it sold, and the balance was made up in gold and silver.[10]

Tibet's relation with British India:

The English were aware of some of the commercial possibilities of Tibet from the moment when they first set foot on the Indian subcontinent, but they took no steps to develop trade across the Himalayas until, in the years following the battle of Plassey, they found themselves in control of territory stretching from the Bay of Bengal to the foothills of the mountain barrier to the north.

Before the signing of the treaty of Nanking in 1842, British dealings with China were confined to trade at Canton. Hence, not surprisingly, in the 18th and 19th centuries attempts were made to develop Anglo-Chinese relations across the Himalayan Mountain. The possibility of a route across the Himalayas for the introduction of British manufactures especially British woollen textiles into the Chinese Empire received serious consideration during this period. Attempts to sell

---

[10] Ibid

such goods at Canton had been disappointing. Hence, the British efforts were to use Tibet as a backdoor to China.

<u>Trade Routes:</u>

No mediaeval trade routes ever crossed Tibet from the north. Along the length of the intervening plains of Chinese Turkestan they ran westward from China till they touched the central barrier (the Taurus of the Classics), which is the eastern wall of the Pamir. They then diverged north-ward, or twisted over the Pamir region to Badakshan and the Oxus, but they ever avoided Tibet. The countless tides of Central Asian emigrates like Aryans, Skyths, Mongols etc., when they overflowed into India, passed by way of Badakshan and the Hindu Kush, never across Tibet. No Chinese pilgrim seeking knowledge at the fountain-head in northern India ever traced his way across the Tibetan uplands from the plains of western china and Kashgar, although he often selected a straighter route than that of Mongol invaders. Avoiding the central Pamir region and Tibet by crossing the Hindu Kush near its north-eastern base by either the Wakijir or Baroghel pass, he entered the valleys of Gilgit and Chitral in order to make his way over routes incredibly rough and difficult to the ancient Gandhara- the seat of all that was most sacred to Buddhism in the extreme north-west of India. The great rolling Tibetan highlands have thus played a most important role in history of Asiatic migration. They have been the natural buffer-land between Central Asia and India, covering so wide a space of the northern frontiers of India, that the only mountain gateways that have ever been opened from the north into the rich sunlit plains of the peninsula are to be found beyond them, and within the comparatively restricted length of the mountain borderland which stretches between Karachi and Kohistan of Kabul.

The traveller who wishes to traverse the wide desolation of the Tibetan plateau has a considerable choice of routes. From north, south, east and the west explorers and adventures have tackled the problem of reaching the capital of the country, Lhasa, and with about equal want to success. The northern routes from the plains of Chinese Turkestan which have been exploited by Prjevalski, Sven Hedin, Deasy, Stein, Littledale, Bonvalot, and others are distinctly the most difficult and unpromising, partly because it is necessary to reach the plains of Kashgar before attempting them- and this in itself is no mean performance; partly because these northern routes lead to the wildest and most desolate uplands of all the desolate field which Tibet presents. These are Russian routes, inasmuch as they lead directly from the Russian Asiatic borderland of Chinese Turkestan, and they are long routes, bristling with all the formidable barriers that a bleak and immensely high mountain system can set in their way before the dreary open steppe than those of Southern Tibet. Russia is shut off from the capital of Tibet by natural barriers which are infinitely greater than those which present themselves on the side of India. Geographically, Lhasa, and all of Tibet which holds promise of future civilised development, within the meshes of the broad network of hinterland communication which is cast from India or from China , and never could be attached to a direct northern system by any but the weakest of geographical ties. There is nevertheless a bond of religious and commercial union between Russia and Tibet which is maintained by a much-traversed route on the northeast, a long route and an important one, about which there is more to be said hereafter.

From the south Tibet is approached by the Sutlej opening through the Himalayas and by a group of passes leading from Kumaon. There are also routes about which we know little leading direct from Nepal, but the principal groups of trans-Himalayan passes into Tibet are those which traverse the valleys of Sikkim and Bhutan.

On the east one or two routes are well known, amongst them one which from prehistoric days has been the main and the best-trodden route from china to Lhasa, i.e., that which cuts the boundary at the frontier station of Ta-chien-lu (Darchendo). This indeed not only connects Peking with Lhasa, and is historically responsible for the great movement of the Chinese race westward which ended in the conquest of Tibet, but it stretches its length to Kashmir and India, and must rank as one of the greatest of Asiatic trade routes.

The routes into Tibet from the north-west diverge from leh, the capital of Ladakh, and many a traveller has started from that quaint Buddhist town in search of adventure in the trackless Tibetan plateau land. Ladakh is the extreme outlying, uptilted province of Kashmir, and the modern road between Srinagar and Leh is a well-laid-out route two hundred and forty miles in length, frequently traversed, but involving some formidable passes. Leaving behind him the sober shade of the thick pine woods of the Sind valley, the traveller encounters the main orographical line of division between Kashmir and Tibet at the point marked by the well-known Zoji La pass, "a pass which is typical of many other Himalayan passes, where the cutting back of the southern stream at its head has tended to obliterate the steep slopes of the northern side. From his experience of approaching it from the Tibetan side, the great traveller Sven Hedin calls it "the worst pass I have ever seen," although its altitude is low compared to many other ones which he must have previously encountered in Tibet.

Beyond the Zoji La the road drops into the Indus basin, and is within the limits of Ladakh, which geographically and climatically belongs rather to Tibet than to Kashmir. Near Leh the Indus is walled in between tremendous precipices, where it has literally carved a way for itself through the mountains. Leh is the market town, the commercial centre of western Tibet. The town climbs up the side of a hill, as do most Tibetan towns, and the general look of it, flat-topped as to roofs and sloping as to walls, is almost Chinese in effect; but it lacks the grace of Chinese outline.

Farther east again we find a group of passes connecting Kumaon with Tibet to the north of Almorah, the Mana, Niti, Milam, Darma, and Byans, all forking off from the upper tributaries of the Alaknanda affluent of the Ganges. All these passes appear to be over eighteen thousand feet. Across the Milam there is still some traffic in gold-dust and borax, which is brought across the Himalayas on the backs of sheep, which still continue to be the beasts of burden in southern Tibet. They travel remarkably well, and keep their condition under circumstances which would prove fatal to the condition of mules.[11] They take back to Tibet cooking-utensils, pots, pans, and earthenware, but naturally no very bulky merchandise can be transported over the rugged mountain tracks in this way.

The Karali, or Gogra river rising near the sources of the Sutlej and Indus, also affords a trans-Himalayan passage; but it leads through a maze of mountains to the same focus on which the more western routes converge, and has apparently no separate trade outlet of its own on to the Tibetan plateau. All these routes practically

---

[11] Sir Thomas Holdich, Tibet, The Mysterious, Alston Rivers Limited London, P. 21.

centre on the same point, the twin lakes of Manasarawar in the southern Tibetan district of Nari Khurasam, or Hundes, which lie below the sacred peaks of Kailas. The great alluvial plain of Nari Khursam divided by the gorge of the Sutlej River is a sort of landing in the Tibetan staircase. In its midst totling is the chief place of importance, as we shall see further on.

The most significant group of passes leading from India into Tibet is that of Sikkim, connecting the basins of the Tista and of the Ammu Chu (river of Assam) with the valley of the Tsanpo near Lhasa.

Two or three routes into Tibet diverge from our railway base at Siliguri on the eastern frontier. One is carried by the mountain railway line to Darjiling; and from Darjiling as his base the traveller descends into the Tista valley, and makes his way by an easily recognisable, but occasionally difficult, route along the Lachen affluent of the Tista and over the Kamba La or Kangra Pass to Kamba Jong. Kamba jong is separated from the trade and religious centre of Shinatze on the Tsanpo by cross-country roads, for the most part no better and no worse than the ordinary unmade country tracks passing through the uncultivated areas of India, but with one or two crossings of mountains passes en route. Some travellers may take the Lach lung affluent to the Donkia pass and strike into the road to Gyangtse. This route, however, involves five or six crossings of intermediate passes before reaching Gyangtse, and although such passes are not formidable, they are obstructive. By far the most direct route to Gyangtse and Lhasa is that which was followed by the Tibetan mission under Colonel Younghusband. From Siliguri a cart road runs by the Tista valley to Kalimpong, just below Darjiling, and thence diverges to the northeast over a series of ascents and descents for forty-two miles to Gnathong, and on to the "smooth and easy" pass called Jelep La, which divides the basin of the Tista from the upper basin of the Ammo Chu or Chumbi, which is Tibet. At this point only Tibet drives a wedge southward into the body of the Himalayas. The valley of the Ammo Chu formerly belonged to Bhutan, but Tibet has recently asserted the right of occupation, and it is here that her troublesome intrusions into British territory necessitated the campaign of 1888, which succeeded in driving the Tibetan rabble over the Jelep La into Chumbi, from whence they came.

Chumbi is said to be a delightful country. It has been called the Engradine of the Himalayas, and it is doubtless a pleasant offset to the wintry regions which lie above and beyond it. Pari, in the upper valley, is a town of about three hundred houses, protected by a fort. It is an important trade entrepot, where tobacco, fruit, and cloth from Bhutan are found, together with vegetables, cattle, and fish. Customs are collected here by Tibetan officials. The Tang La, above Pari, is an exceptionally easy pass for the Himalayas. From it northward there runs a stream which, swelling into a stream and finally developing into a full-grown river, flows almost directly northward through an open and gently rounded plain to Gyangtse and the Yeru Tsanpo. The great central route across the breadth of southern Tibet, -that part of Tibet which, being within the Brahmaputra basin, is in true geographical affinity with India in spite of the intervening Himalayan wall. The journey from the Indian frontier to Lhasa may be made in a fortnight over fairly good country roads and through tracts which are partially cultivated. From the north, from Kashgar or the frontier of Chinese Turkestan to Lhasa, it is a journey of months across a wild and desolate table-land, the horrors of which have been described to us by Sven Hedin, Bower,

Prjevalski, and others, presenting as aspect of Tibet which has little in common with the Tibet of the upper Brahmaputra.

Setting aside for the present certain routes through Bhutan to Lhasa, we may note that there are yet other ways into Tibet than those of the west and south and east, and by these other ways adventurers have reached the plateau from the north.

Tibetan prejudice against travellers was too much for them. But they all scaled the northern walls of Tibet, and we know that there is not one, but several, recognised passes from the lowlands of Chinese Turkestan to the highlands of the plateau, which even in their rough condition of natural obstructiveness are yet passable for horses and camels.

The trade between Tibet and its southern neighbours has been carried out since ancient times. The lure of trans-Himalayan trade was Lhasa: India and Tibet were the principal partners while Nepal formed the principal venue through which this trade was conducted. It was in the seventh century A.D. that the emergence of powerful Tibetan Kingdom with its capital at Lhasa transformed Kathmandu Valley into the intellectual and commercial entrepot between India and central Asia. It appears that only limited trade was carried out during the next several centuries.[12]

Throughout the remote ages, Tibet and Nepal communicated with each other through the 24 high passes (averaging 17,000 feet). The lowest of these are the historic Kuti and Kerong passes with elevations of 6,000 feet, located at Kodari and Rasuwa respectively. The other important passes are located at Takla, Mustang; Hati and Wallanchung. It was through these passes that Nepal exported to Tibet food grains in exchange for gold, salt, wool, sheep, goats and yak-tails. The two passes of Kutiand

---

[12] Rose, L.E., Nepal-Strategy for Survival, Univ. of California, Berkeley, 1971, p. 10.

Kerong were often a source of dispute between Nepal and Tibet from the medieval period to modern times.[13]

Trading Commodities:

Whilst the gates of Tibet have ever been jealously guarded against European advance from the west or south, and the wild, bleak wind-swept plains and rocky defiles of the northwest, with the desolation of dreary steppes, stretching in stone-strewn monotony for hundreds of miles, have effectually hindered the progress of trade developments in these directions through all historic times, it has not been the same on the east or the northeast. From the west, in spite of all obstacles, a certain amount of intermittent trade has always filtered through Leh, or over the passes of Kumaon to India owing chiefly to the fact that gold and borax are easily transportable commodities; but the trade of Tibet has always run China-wards. Gold, even from the extreme western field near the Kashmir border, has been carried in far larger quantities to Peking, over a distance of three thousand miles, than it ever has to Leh, which is hardly three hundred miles from the centre of the western mining districts. The Sikhs, by way of Kashmir, and the Mongols, from the north, have alike attempted the conquest of Tibet with no substantial commercial profit; but the Chinese from the east have swamped the country with most practical results. Trade and commerce either follow the flag, or precede it, and most of the material comforts and luxuries of the few centres of semi-civilisation which Tibet possesses are the direct result of Chinese military enterprise. Tea, for instance, of an especially inferior quality, made as much from refuse as from the actual leaf, and cemented with rice

---

[13] Uprety, P.R., Nepal-Tibet Relations 1850-1930, Paga Nara, Kathmandu, 1980, p. 2.

water into the form of hard unpromising bricks, is imported in immense quantities from china, and, strange to say, it fully meets the requirements and the taste of a people who do not appreciate Indian tea.[14]

On April 29, 1954 the agreement between the people's Republic of China and the Republic of India on trade and communications between the Tibet region of China and India was signed in Peking, according to a Chinese communiqué, bringing to an end the remnant privileges of the British and so establishing the relations between China and India, concerning Tibet, on a new basis. The agreement laid down five broad principles in addition to the liquidation of the Indian claims.

<u>Tibetan Medicine:</u>

The Tibetan system of Medicine, known as *Swa Rigpa* (the Art of Healing) is an interesting example showing India's influence on the culture of Tibet and the constant interactions between the two nations. As for all Tibetan traditional sciences, the medical system is said to originate from the Buddha Sakyamuni himself. However, the Tibetan historical texts, particularly *The Survey of Tibetan Medical History* written by the Regent Desi Sangye Gyatso during the 18th century differs very little from the Vedic texts expounding the history of the Ayurveda. The only difference is that Buddha takes the place of Vedic rishis as the originator of the medical system. The history of the Tibetan system of medicine is usually classified into three categories.

1. The spread of Medicine in the God Realm

2. The spread of Medicine in the Human Realm (in India)

---

[14] Sir Thomas Holdich, Tibet, The Mysterious, Alston Rivers Limited London, p. 26-27.

3. The spread of Medicine in Tibet.

In the spread of medicine in the God realm, the customary in-fighting between gods, the churning of the ocean in which is hidden the ambrosia of immortality, the using of Mt Meru as stirring rod, the encounter between the Buddha and Brahma and the final recovery of the ambrosia are recounted. In the Tibetan tradition, it is Brahma who receives the teachings from Buddha: the medical science is thus transmitted through a text known as *The 100,000 Verses of Healing*.

The history of the origin of Tibetan medicine is closely mixed with events of the Buddha's life such as the sermon on the Four Noble Truths or some other teachings at the Venture Peak near Rajagriha. The Tibetan texts also record the life and teachings of Jivaka, a famous doctor who lived at the same time as Buddha and became one of his disciples. Nagarjuna is said to be the author of several treatises on medicine. His knowledge was transmitted to Asvaghosa who himself wrote several books, the best known being the *Astanga-hrdaya-samhita* (The Eight Branches) which is still today a reference for the medical students. During the reign of King Songtsen-Gompo, physicians and medical experts from India, China, Central Asia and Persia were requested to bring their own system of medicine (it is said that some even came from Greece6). A century later, the famous physician Yuthok Yonten Gompo the Elder thrice visited India and later compiled the Gyud Shi (or Four Tantras) which is still today the base of the Tibetan medical knowledge. Using Indian medical scriptures, it incorporated some features of the other systems, particularly the indigenous system of Tibet. A very original and well adapted *Art of Healing* was born.

After six visits, Yuthok Yonten Gompo the Younger, who lived in the 12th century completed in India, the work of Yuthok the Elder (he is said to be his reincarnation). The 156 Chapters of the Gyud Shi are still considered as the essence of Tibetan medical knowledge and are studied as such not only in Tibet, but also by the Tibetans in exile in India and the local Amchis (medical practitioners) in the Himalayan region. It is worth noting that *Astanga-hrdaya-samhita* still exists not only in its Tibetan translation (dating from Rinchen Zangpo's time), but also in its original Sanskrit version. It is a unique occasion to study both versions and marvel at the quality of the translation. It also helps to establish terminological parallels between both languages and shows the proximity of both literatures.

Being desirous of promoting trade and cultural intercourse between Tibet Region of China and India and of facilitating pilgrimage and travel by the peoples if China and India, the two countries have resolved to enter into the present Agreement[15] based on the following principles:

1. Mutual respect for each other's territorial integrity and sovereignty.

2. Mutual non-aggression.

3. Mutual non-interference in each other's internal affairs.

4. Equality and mutual benefit.

5. Peaceful co-existence.

According to the agreement India accepted the principle that Tibet constituted an integral part of China, and agreed to withdraw completely within six months the Indian contingent that had been stationed for decades at Tatung and Gyantse. Peking,

---

[15] Sino-Indian Trade Agreement over Tibetan Border, 29th APRIL, 1954.

it was stated, would render all assistance and facilities in aiding the withdrawal of Indian troops.

India also agreed to hand over all her property in Tibet to the Chinese authorities, leaving questions of detail regarding cost and manner of payment to be worked out later. These properties included all the telegraph public telephone, and postal establishments, together with their equipments and twelve rest houses situated in various parts of Tibet.

For more than 50 years, India has been a sometimes gracious, sometimes uneasy and occasionally hostile host to tens of thousands of Tibetans who fled their homeland and settled here after claiming religious and political persecution by the Chinese government.

For India, which has been sometimes criticized for an ostrich-like "non-alignment" approach to foreign policy, the situation represents an unusually sophisticated balancing act. India has allowed generations of Tibetans to build a miniature Tibet within the country, and officials express sympathy for the Tibetan cause. But maintaining a growing economic relationship with China is vital, analysts and political experts say.

Political experts in India have been openly critical of China's handling of Tibetans' quest for autonomous rule and their desire to preserve an independent culture, while pragmatic about the need to forge good relations with China.

Since the Dalai Lama first fled China in 1959 to India after a failed Tibetan uprising, India has maintained a nuanced position. "The Indian government, while sympathetic to the case of the Dalai Lama, contends that Tibet legally is a part of China," an article from The New York Times in September 1959 reported. Flash forward to 2006, the last time Indian and Chinese heads of state made a joint statement about Tibet:

"The Indian side reiterates that it has recognized the Tibet Autonomous Region as part of the territory of the People's Republic of China, and that it does not allow Tibetans to engage in anti-China political activities in India. The Chinese side expresses its appreciation for the Indian position."

India's uneasy hospitality does not come without some advantages for India, political analysts say. India has informally agreed with China not to allow its officials to meet with the Dalai Lama or share a stage with him, but that is sometimes broached. "Whenever there is a problem between India and China, India plays the *Tibet card*," said Srikanth Kondapalli, the chairman for East Asian Studies at Jawaharlal Nehru University. "When China indulges in anti-Indian activities, the Indian foreign secretaries meet the Dalai Lama," he said.

CHAPTER II

INDIA'S RELATIONS WITH TIBET
AFTER INDIAN INDEPENDENC IN 1947

As India became a sovereign nation after in 1947, it is the time to take a pause to reflect on the policies of the past, to revisit its triumphs, its failures and to reflect on challenges met and opportunities lost.

The macro picture that emerged is of great success. Following a distressing and violent partition, and burdened with a colonial economy drained by 200 years of exploitation, India in 1947 faced an uncertain future. But today India boasts of a strong demographically young society and a $4 Trillion economy set on the path of irreversible growth. It is taken for granted that India will be a major player in the new global balance of power.

And yet, as India celebrates her success, it's needed to introspect and identify the areas where it missed the mark. If anyone asked to name a single issue on which India failed to measure up to its challenges the unhesitating answer will be that it is Tibet. And such wisdom behind sight is important because it ensures that the errors of judgment of the past will not be repeated. What had gone wrong with India's Tibetan policy? These are some possible answers:

1. India's assumption that China was interested in larger issues like joining India in creating an Asian renaissance turned out to be entirely incorrect.

2. Under a policy described by former foreign secretary Mr. Jagat Mehta as "Unilateral Friendliness" with China, India blindly believed the false

assurances of the Chinese leaders that the Chinese maps of our northern borders were cartographic errors and they would be rectified soon. In fact they were never rectified.

3. Equally honestly India believed the Chinese assurances regarding the safety of the Dalai Lama and the welfare of the Tibetan People but China has never been serious about this.

4. In the subsequent negotiations with China on the border issue, it was wrong in taking a rigid, legalistic posture and asserting territorial claims for which there was insufficient evidence. The jury is still out on the assertion of Mr. A.G. Noorani that all our claims were not entirely founded by empirical evidences.

5. The Tibetan issue reflects a major systemic failure at India's end. There were voices within the cabinet that were urging caution in dealing with China - amongst them two home ministers; Sardar Patel and Pandit Govind Ballabh Pant and finance minister Morarji Desai. Their advice was ignored. India's national interests would have been better protected if Pandit Nehru had taken his cabinet colleagues to his meeting with Chou En Lai in February 1960.

In 1950, when PLA troops entered Lhasa, not only did India do nothing, it dissuaded the UN and other countries that were willing to come to the rescue of the Tibetans. In 1951, when the so-called 17 point agreement was forced on the adverse government of the Dalai Lama, India did not protest. In 1954, India signed an agreement with China under which it surrendered all its rights and responsibilities in Tibet and withdrew its garrisons from Yatung and Shigatse. That the 1954 agreement was signed in the name of the Buddhist principles of the *Panchsheela* made it a tragic mockery of the Tibetan people.

After India has irrevocably surrendered its 'Tibet Card' and formally accepted Chinese sovereignty over Tibet, the question is whether anything can be done for the Tibetan people by India or by the international community?

There is a growing body of opinion that in a global and interdependent world, the concept of state sovereignty is no longer absolute. The talk is increasingly about a "responsible sovereignty" or "shared sovereignty". No state in the world today can claim the absolute, sovereign right to deny basic human rights and freedom to its own citizens. In extreme circumstances, and subject to transparent and credible safeguards, the international community can also exercise the Right to Protect to affected groups.

The Tibetan uprising and the Role of the Dalai Lama:

In order to obtain a correct perspective of the events leading up to the flight of the Dalia Lama from Tibet and his arrival in India on March 31st, 1959, It is necessary to examine the important facts and events from 1951 to 1959 behind it. Although there is nothing in the Seven-Point Agreement to suggest that Tibet was to be carved up. Tibet was in fact divided into three parts, one of which was put under the control of Chamdo Liberation Committee headed by General Wang Chi Mei, a Chinese General, the second under the Panchen Lama's Bureau and the third, which came to be described as the local government, was nominally under the jurisdiction of the Dalai Lama and his Government.

The Dalai Lama in his Tezpur Statement has mentioned that the "Tibetan Government did not enjoy any measure of autonomy even in internal matters and the Chinese Government exercised full powers in Tibetan affairs". In his press statement[16] of June 20th, 1959, he said:

"Although they had solemnly undertaken to maintain my status and power as the Dalai Lama, they did not lose any opportunity to undermine my authority and sow dissensions among my people. In fact, they compelled me, situated as I was, to dismiss my Prime Ministers under threat of their execution without trial, because they had in all honesty and sincerity resisted the unjustified usurpations of power by representatives of the Chinese Government in Tibet.

"Far from carrying out the agreement they deliberately began to pursue a course of policy which was diametrically opposed to the terms and conditions which they had themselves laid down. Thus, commenced a reign of terror, which finds few parallels in the history of Tibet. Forced labor and compulsory exaction of certain leading men in Tibet, these are the glorious achievements of the Chinese rule in Tibet".

At about the end of 1955 uprisings look place in the north-eastern and eastern regions of Tibet, which were under the Chamdo Liberation Committee and the Panchen Lama's Bureau. Soon these uprisings spread westwards. In 1956 the Dalai Lama visited India and remained in India till April 1957. Little was known at the time of the serious situation in Tibet and the extremely difficult position in which the

---

[16] Deb Bahadur Thapa, Tibet Past and Present Human Violations in Tibet, Vol. 3, p. 68.

Dalai Lama found himself. The Dalai Lama in his press statement of June 20th, 1959 stated,

> "As I was unable to do anything for the benefit of my people I had practically made up my mind when I came to India not to return to Tibet until there was a manifest change in the attitude of the Chinese authorities. I therefore sought the advice of the Prime Minister of India who has always shown me unfailing kindness and consideration. After his talk with the Chinese Prime Minister and on the strength of the assurance given by him on behalf of China, Mr. Nehru advised me to change my decision."

Mr. Nehru in his speech in the Indian Parliament of April 27th, 1959, has confirmed that he did give such advice to the Dalai Lama on the assurances he had received from Mr. Chou En Lai, who had been on a visit to India in December, 1956.

In 1957 the situation had worsened and evidently, in an attempt to pacify the outraged Tibetan sentiments, Mao Tse Tung, in his well known 'Hundred Flowers Speech' said that reforms would not be introduced in Tibet during the period of 1958-62 and that thereafter the introduction of reforms would depend on the wishes of the Tibetan people.

<u>Flight of the Dalai Lama</u>:

The Dalai Lama had received an invitation from China's military commander to attend a cultural programme on March 10th, 1959 at the military headquarters; he was asked to come unaccompanied by any of his ministers or his bodyguard. Earlier, a number of Lamas namely Head Lama Amdo-Sharkelden Gyalto, Head Lama Amdo-Kunchok Lhundup and Lama Kham-Pandit Shi Chen were killed and Lama

Kathok Situ was imprisoned. In this situation, a large number of people surrounded the Norbulinga Palace, where the Dalai Lama was in residence. All the ministers except one gathered in the palace. The exception was a minister who was considered to be pro-Chinese who was prevented by the people from entering the palace. People continued to stay round the Palace throughout the night of the 10th March.

On 11th March 1959 a meeting of all Government officials was called at the palace, a few Pro-Chinese officials did not attend and a proclamation was issued in the name of the cabinet that Tibet was independent.   About 5000 women also gathered and asked the Dalai Lama to proclaim Tibet's independence.

On 12th March a large meeting was held at Shol, below the Potala Palace. Almost the whole population of Lhasa seems to have been present. At this meeting it was decided to prepare documents regarding the claim of independence. A letter was sent to Mr. Shakabpa, mentioning these facts and he was asked to announce to the world the facts about the Chinese oppression and the decision of the Tibetan people regarding independence. This meeting was almost in continuous session between 12th and the 17th of March and the people gathered were entirely unarmed. But the letter never reached Mr. Shakabpa.

During night two shells were fired on the Palace but fell in an artificial lake in front of the Palace. Machine-gun firing was heard. Thereafter the Dalai Lama and some of his party left the Palace to India one by one. The shells were evidently fired by the Chinese as a warning in the hope of getting the Dalai Lama to surrender. On the early morning of the19th a series bombardment of the Palace began. The Chinese were not aware that Dalai Lama had left 24 hours earlier. The bombardment greatly damaged the Norbulinga Palace and other parts of the city. It created terror among the people. Large number of refugees lost their life.

The struggle was continued. On the basis of the Tibetan sources the Chinese claim that the revolt has been put down does not seem to be justified, excepting in so far as the area in and around Lhasa was concerned. In an interview given by the Dalai Lama to Mr. Mahesh Chandra, special correspondent of the *Statesman* (India) on June 6th, 1959, the Dalai Lama (former) stated that the news from Tibet he had lately received was sad to the extreme. There was much trouble for his people. Every day he heard of fresh atrocities. He appealed to the editor of this newspaper to help in bringing the terrible happenings in Tibet to public notice.

He further said that both the Tibetans who had remained behind and those who had come away were suffering equally, the first physically and the second mentally. "But we both feel the same pain. Those who are left behind are being subjected to unbearable tortures day and night". He ended by saying, "Despite all these difficulties, and come what may, our spirit will never die. Tibet will live. One day our beloved country will arrive at the journey's end, when truth shall triumph".

Nature of the Uprising:

As to the nature of the uprising the Chinese have claimed that it has all been engineered or organized by the upper class reactionaries. By the end of May 1959, there were about 15000 refugees in India and many were in Sikkim, Nepal, and Bhutan. Enquiries show that the refugees were not what have been described by communist China as "reactionaries", but the overwhelming majorities were the common people.

The leaders of the rebellion have banded themselves in an organization called "Ten-Soung-Ma-Ghar", viz. the National Voluntary Defence Army of Tibet. A reference to the National Voluntary Defence Army has been made by the Dalai Lama in his news conference. A recent statement by the leaders of this army discloses that on January 1, 1959 a declaration made by them set out radical changes in the social and political organization of the country. The proposals include acquisition of large landed estates on payment of compensation, the introduction of the elective system on the basis of adult suffrage and the principles of individual liberty according to modern constitutional concept. They have stated,

> "We pledge ourselves for the improvement of the condition of our people and their standard of living. We engage ourselves to introduce all necessary reforms in the country in accordance with the natural conditions, customs and genius of our people. In the field of economic development we pledge ourselves to improve the life of our nomadic people, of the tillers of the land, of the artisans and the handicrafts men to the best of our ability and to effect changes in all spheres of our national life. It is our declared policy to bring about these changes by peaceful means."

To counter the imminent Communist Chinese onslaught the Kashag (the Parliament), led by Regent Takdrak, sought help from the few countries that had relations with Tibet. In November 1949 Tibet communicated with the US and Britain seeking their diplomatic and military support in the event of Chinese invasion. In addition, Tibet requested the US, Britain and India to help Tibet to obtain United Nations (UN) membership on the ground that these countries shared a history of close relations with Tibet. But Tibet did not receive any commitment from these countries.[17]

The government of Tibet, in utmost urgency, convened the National Assembly. The assembly came to the conclusion that Tibet could not match the PRC if Tibet were to engage in a military confrontation with China. Still the National Assembly was under no delusion that the sovereignty of Tibet must be safeguarded at any cost, so it proposed to send missions to Britain, the US, India and Nepal to seek their help to resist the Chinese invasion. The Kashag appointed four delegates and sent messages of their coming visits to the countries. But these countries refused to receive the Tibetan delegates.[18]

In mid-1950 the Tibetan delegation received a communiqué from the Secretary-General of the Central People's Government of the PRC, Lin Boqu, stating that place of negotiation should be Beijing, and that the Tibetan delegates should bear in mind that they represented the local Tibetan government. Thus they could not call themselves diplomats of Tibet. The Tibetan delegation remained in India for over one year trying to obtain visas to travel to Hong Kong, and later to work out a preliminary negotiation with the Ambassador of the PRC to New Delhi. But they failed in their endeavours due to lack of favourable foreign support and other reasons.

The Battle of Chamdo:

With so many insurmountable hurdles coming on their way the Tibetan delegation was left to shuttle between the offices of the Indian foreign ministry and embassies of the PRC and other western countries. The PRC saw this as a tactic

---

[17] B. R. Deepak, India and China, 2005, p. 123-124.
[18] 14th Dalai Lama, *My Land and My People* 1962, p.89.

employed by the Tibetan delegates to drag their feet and take the PRC for a ride. So on 6 October 1950 the PLA waged a full-scale war on Chamdo, which lasted till 24 October, resulting in the complete defeat of the ill-equipped Tibetan army and capture of Ngabo, who had just recently replaced Lhalu as the Governor-General of Chamdo.

Tibet Appeals to the United Nations:

At that time the Korean War was a major global concern. And the UN was actively intervening in the Korean War. Tibet saw rays of hope that the UN might as well come to the rescue of Tibet in the face of Chinese invasion. So on 7 November 1950 Tibet appealed to the UN to help counter Chinese invading forces, though the government of India advised Tibet not to do so.

The United Nations General Committee debated the issue of whether to include the invasion of Tibet by foreign forces as an additional item in the UN General Assembly on 24 November 1950. Neither Britain who was largely responsible for the present Tibetan situation nor India who had inherited the British legacy in Tibet supported the Tibetan appeal. Tibet found an unexpected supporter in El Salvador, a small republic in Latin America.[19]

Hector David Castro, the El Salvador representative to the UN, made a case for a draft resolution to be passed on the Tibetan case in the UN General Committee, but representatives of Britain and India spoke vehemently against it and other representatives including that of the US did not support the resolution. Thus Tibet found itself left to its own fate, once again.

---

[19] B R Deepak *op. Cit.* p. 136-137.

The Dalai Lama Assumes Power:

After having lost Chamdo to the invading Chinese forces, with no international help forthcoming, the whole atmosphere in Lhasa was one of fear and anxiety. Regent Takdrak and other senior officials convened meetings to find a solution to the crisis. The Tibetan National Assembly requested Regent Takdrak to pass the rein of the country to the Dalai Lama. Even the state oracles, Nechung and Gadhong, seconded the proposal. At that time the Dalai Lama was only 16, two years short of the minimum age at which earlier Dalai Lamas had assumed both spiritual and temporal power of Tibet. Over and above, the Dalai Lama had much unfinished religious studies to pursue. So initially, citing his young age the Dalai Lama declined the offer[20]. Because of the crisis in the country and people's unanimous faith in his leadership, the Dalai Lama had to give in to repeated appeals from the members of the Kashag and the National Assembly.

On 17 November 1950 the Dalai Lama assumed both spiritual and political authority of Tibet. As soon as he assumed full power, the Dalai Lama sent a letter to the Chinese leadership through the commander of the Chinese army that invaded Chamdo. In the letter the Dalai Lama informed the Chinese leadership that he had assumed full power in Tibet and wished for better relations between Tibet and China. He asked the PRC to release all Tibetan prisoners of war captured in the Chamdo battle and return all territories occupied by Chinese forces.[21]

At this point in time the atmosphere in Lhasa was tense with growing apprehension that the invading Chinese army might soon storm the holy city. So the

---

[20] 14th Dalai Lama, *My Land and My People*, p. 91.
[21] Ibid p. 93-94.

Kashag yet again convened a National Assembly meeting, which vehemently proposed that the Tibetan administration be shifted to Dromo on the ground that the Dalai Lama's safety was of utmost importance. Dromo was located a short distance away from the Tibet-India border, and the Dalai Lama and his government could easily escape to India in case the PLA invaded further into the heartland of Tibet.

So the Dalai Lama accompanied by his senior officials, left Lhasa on 19 December 1950 and on 7 January 1951 the Dalai Lama and major organs of the government of Tibet were relocated to Dromo[22]

Meanwhile at Chamdo, Ngabo was still a prisoner in the hands of the Chinese. There he was made to receive forced Communist Education. At Dromo the Dalai Lama received a letter from Ngabo, which in fact was a creation of Wang Qimei, the commanding officer of the Chinese army that invaded Chamdo. Ngabo's letter was not drafted by Ngabo himself. It was dictated by Wang Qimei[23]. The letter advised the Dalai Lama that Tibet had no alternative but to engage in peaceful negotiation with the Chinese. On the part of the Chinese, they promised they would not move an inch forward from where they were stationed. Ngabo, a very decisive administrator, showed no hesitation in offering himself as the negotiator, if the Government of Tibet found it agreeable. As Ngabo volunteered to shoulder the responsibility of negotiating with the Chinese the Dalai Lama agreed to his proposal and appointed him as the chief negotiator[24]. At the same time a team of four other delegates and two translators was constituted to assist Ngabo. After a lot of uncertainties over the venue of the negotiations, Tibetan negotiators left for Beijing

---

[22] Warren W. Smith, Jr. *Tibetan Nation* 1997, p. 292.
[23] Ibid p.142-43.
[24] 14th Dalai Lama, *Freedom in Exile* 1990, p. 67.

in two teams. One left from Chamdo by road and the other, from Dromo, via India and Hong Kong.

The 17-Point Agreement:

Before Tibetan delegates left from Dromo the government of Tibet explicitly instructed that Tibet should remain independent, not a word of Tibet becoming part of China should be said. But in case of utter helplessness they were authorized to accept China's external rule over Tibet, provided Tibet enjoyed internal independence. The PRC may commission a consul and a few officials in Tibet, but they should not be more than a hundred in number. The PRC cannot deploy soldiers in Tibet. The Chinese consul should preferably be a devout Buddhist. Most importantly Tibetan delegates should establish telegram link with Dromo as soon as they reached Beijing[25].

As soon as the members of the two groups of Tibetan delegates met each other in Beijing they found themselves literally captives in the hands of the PRC. In Beijing Hotel, where Tibetan delegates were lodged during the negotiation, they had no liberty to receive guests other than Chinese officials. They were not even allowed to go outside the hotel on errands, on the pretext that their lives were at risk. Thus, they were literally confined in the hotel. When Tibetan delegates went outside the hotel under unavoidable circumstances, their movements were monitored closely by Chinese agents.

Before the actual rounds of negotiation began, Chinese representatives wanted the government of Tibet to recognize the Panchen Lama, whom the Chinese had

---

[25] *Biography of the 14th Dalai Lama*, Norbulingka Institute Vol. III 2009, p. 468-469.

recognized some time earlier. Tibetan delegates refused to entertain the request on the ground that they did not have the authority to do so. At that time there were two other prospective candidates of the Panchen Lama in Tibet. Thus, the Tibetan government decided to place the PRC's candidate among the pool of prospective candidates of the Panchen Lama.

The real Panchen Lama had to be chosen through proper religious procedures, and the Dalai Lama had to bless the new reincarnation. During the negotiation the PRC's candidate was in Beijing at the invitation of the PRC to assist in the negotiation.

The Chinese representatives were adamant that the government of Tibet recognize their candidate as the 10th Panchen Lama. They reasoned that as Mao Zedong had recognized the candidate as the 10th Panchen Lama, the dignity of Mao Zedong as well as that of the government of the PRC would be undermined if the Tibetan government refused to do the same (Warren W. Smith, Jr. *Tibetan Nation* 1997). So Ngabo sent a telegram to the Kashag informing them that the negotiation could not begin if the Government of Tibet did not approve the child-candidate proposed by the Chinese as the real 10th Panchen Lama. Out of compulsion, rather than conviction, the Kashag approved the Chinese candidate as the real 10th Panchen Lama, though many people from the government and monastic communities demanded a thorough and standard examination to be carried out[26].

The issue of the Panchen Lama's recognition was one of the last about which the Tibetan delegation was able to consult with the Tibetan Government at Yatung. The Tibetans initially communicated with Yatung by means of a telegramic code,

---

[26] 14th Dalai Lama, *My Land and My People* 1962, p. 122.

which, they believed, the Chinese were unable to decipher. This appears to have been the case, since the delegates reported that the Chinese asked them what was in their telegrams and, after the Tibetans refused to tell them that they were prohibited any further communication. The delegates were closely guarded at their hotel and at the old Japanese Embassy, where the talks took place, and their contacts were restricted[27].

From then on the Tibetan delegates were literally on their own, with almost zero communication with their Government, and their movements closely monitored by their hosts. The ensuing negotiations resulted in the discussion of only issues the Chinese wanted to settle, in the way the Chinese wanted to. In the process, the Chinese representatives employed tactics of deceit, coercion and threat. For example, in the cases of deployment of the PLA in Tibet, establishment of a military committee in Tibet and inclusion of issues related to the Panchen Lama in the agreement, the Chinese delegates explicitly threatened to "liberate" Tibet with force and told the Tibetan delegates that they were free to go back to Tibet. During the negotiations, views of the two parties were so polarized that there seemed no common ground in sight. So on many occasions there occurred high pitched arguments, but most of the time the Tibetan delegates found themselves at the receiving end of Chinese threats. Thus, the Tibetan delegates ended up conceding to Chinese demands in fear of military occupation of the country.

The 17-Point Agreement had a lengthy preamble, on which no prior discussion whatsoever was held during the negotiation. Just a day or two before the actual signing of the agreement, a draft of the preamble was given to the Tibetan

---

[27] Warren W. Smith, Jr. *Tibetan Nation* 1997, p. 295.

delegates. It was the first time the Tibetan delegates saw the preamble. Because the preamble was a whimsical interpretation of Tibetan history by the Chinese to suit their interest, Tibetan delegates made a strong case for not including it in the document. But the Chinese authorities never heeded to the Tibetan appeal.

On 23 May 1951 a ceremony was held in Beijing under the patronage of Vice-Chairman of the People's Government, Zhu De, and the Agreement of the Central People's Government and the Local Government of Tibet on Measures for the Peaceful Liberation of Tibet and its appendices were signed by the members of the two parties. Before putting their names on the document, the Tibetan delegates made it clear that they were doing it merely in their individual capacity. They said they were not representing the government of Tibet[28]. They even concealed their personal seals and denied having them on their persons. So the Chinese forged wooden seals bearing names of the Tibetan delegates in Tibetan.

The news of the Tibetan delegates signing the 17-Point Agreement came as a bombshell in Dromo. The Dalai Lama was "transfixed" by it because he had kept the seals of the state with himself at Dromo in order to prevent Ngapo and the other delegates from doing so[29]. Immediately the Dalai Lama telegrammed and instructed Ngabo and his company to send copies of the agreement to Dromo and remain in Beijing until further instructions. But they chose to return, saying that if the Tibetan government wanted to resume the talks, it would be better to send new negotiators[30]. Though the Tibetan delegates had signed the agreement, yet its legal ratification still

---

[28] Micheal van Walt, *The Status of Tibet* 1987, p. 147-48.
[29] The 14th Dalai Lama, *Freedom in Exile* 1990, p. 69.
[30] Marie & Buffetrille, (ed.) *Authenticating Tibet* 2008, p. 67.

depended upon the Tibetan government, because the Tibetan negotiators lacked plenipotentiary powers[31].

The Dalai Lama Returns to Lhasa:

With the conclusion of the 17-Point Agreement the PRC hurriedly appointed Zhang Jinwu as the representative of the PRC to Tibet. He was assigned to leave for Dromo, along with the group of Tibetan delegates who were returning to Dromo via Hong Kong and India, to meet the Dalai Lama.

When things came to this pass the Government of India felt the Sino-Tibetan problem was a closed affair, so they refused to interfere. The British Government, accordingly, advised the Americans to align themselves with the Indian position. However, the Americans were determined to help Tibet as long as the Tibetans clearly rejected the agreement and resisted Chinese invasion. Therefore, they advised the Dalai Lama to denounce the agreement publicly before the arrival of the Chinese representative on Indian soil[32].

At that time Shakapa, the intermediary between the Dalai Lama and the Americans, was living in India. The Dalai Lama telegrammed Shakapa that he had not empowered Ngabo to sign any agreement, so the agreement was not acceptable to Tibet. But until the Dalai Lama heard a thorough report from the Tibetan delegates and met with the Chinese representative to Tibet, he would not publicly reject the agreement[33].

---

[31] Warren W. Smith, Jr. *Tibetan Nation* 1996, p. 301.
[32] Marie & Buffetrille, op.cit. p. 68.
[33] Michael van Walt, op.cit. p. 148-149.

In this testing time the Dalai Lama was flooded with conflicting counsel, though most of them might have come from well meaning people. There were people who believed it would serve Tibet better if the Dalai Lama escaped into exile and spearheaded Tibet's struggle with international help. This view was shared by the government of the US, the Dalai Lama's elder brother Taktser Rinpoche and the Dalai Lama's long time friend Heinrich Harrer. Among Tibetan officials who expressed similar views included Shakapa, Surkhang, Phalha, Namseling etc.

But Tibetan monastic community was in favour of the Dalai Lama returning to Lhasa and negotiating with the Chinese for better terms. Ever since Buddhism flourished in Tibet views of the monastic community enjoyed unparalleled weight in national-decision-making processes. Even the two Prime Ministers, Lobsang Tashi and Lukhangwa, and the Dalai Lama's personal tutor Ling Rinpoche opined that the Chinese would definitely massacre the Tibetan people in case the Dalai Lama escaped into exile. For the sole purpose of convincing the Dalai Lama to return to Lhasa, the abbots of the three monasteries of Drapong, Sera and Gaden travelled all the way from Lhasa to Dromo and made their case to the Dalai Lama[34].

After hearing varied and divergent views the Dalai Lama did not have the luxury of time, but had to make a quick decision. He was worried about his people. Till then the Dalai Lama had not met a Chinese communist official, though he indeed had heard a lot about them. So the Dalai Lama felt that if he left for exile without even meeting a single Chinese communist official and getting a little acquainted with their mentality, he could not imagine what fate awaited the Tibetan masses under Chinese rule. Moreover, the Dalai Lama did not foresee guaranteed support from the

---

[34] The 14th Dalai Lama, *Freedom in Exile* 1990, p. 70-71.

US, because it was still involved in the Korean War and the people of the US might not favour their government taking up the cause of Tibet at the expense of their tax money.

Most importantly, the Dalai Lama abhorred bloodshed. He believed his denunciation of the agreement and accepting the US assistance would most probably mean war with the PRC, which inevitably would result in bloodshed[35]. Therefore, the Dalai Lama decided to wait to hear the reports of the Tibetan delegates and to examine the attitude of the Chinese representative. Over and above, the presence of large contingents of PLA at Chamdo in full battle preparedness might possibly have had the desired effect on the Dalai Lama's mind.

Days later, after having heard reports from the Tibetan delegates and meeting with the Chinese representative, the Dalai Lama felt he could serve his people better if he returned to Lhasa. He intended to personally try to effect changes to some of the articles of the 17-Point Agreement, or to re-negotiate with them a brand new agreement, if possible[36].

The Dalai Lama's return to Lhasa, however may be paradoxical and debatable, indeed calmed the political atmosphere in Tibet. But his return did not in any way stop the PLA marching into central Tibet, that too in large numbers and from different regions. This is partly because the PLA's advancement into central Tibet was a decision that the central PRC leadership had taken much earlier. They intended to execute the plan whether or not the Dalai Lama returned to Lhasa. No sooner the 17-Point Agreement was concluded, even though the document still lacked ratification from the Kashag, than the PRC ordered many PLA units to

---

[35] Ibid, p.70.
[36]. Michael van Walt, op. cit., p. 149

advance to central Tibet from different border regions. Like a magician at work the PLA soldiers virtually flooded central Tibet in large numbers in a short period. But their demeanor was gentle and appeasing, at least for the initial period. Had the Dalai Lama chosen to escape into exile from Dromo, considering what would occur later starting from March 1959, the experienced and well-armed PLA would have shown no hesitation in massacring Tibetans while advancing into central Tibet.

The Dalai Lama's return to Lhasa from Dromo is not an act of accepting the terms of the 17-Point Agreement. After the Dalai Lama returned to Lhasa the PRC's military build-up in central Tibet increased exponentially with each passing day. Consequently the Chinese tone of speech and demeanour towards Tibetan people, and Tibetan leadership in particular turned aggressive and threatening. This was manifested in the fact that two prime ministers of Tibet, Silon Lobsang Tashi and Silon Lukhangwa, were forced to resign and the Chinese leaders started meeting the Dalai Lama directly, sidestepping established official protocol. Therefore, over a period of time the Dalai Lama's desire to effect changes to some of the articles of the 17-Point Agreement, or to re-negotiate a brand new agreement with the Chinese evaporated into thin air. Under the gravity of the situation the National Assembly was hurriedly convened and it recommended the Kashag to agree to the terms of the 17-Point Agreement, provided the PRC clarified on some doubts that the people of Tibet felt concerned about.

Accordingly, the Kashag sought clarification on three issues from the Chinese representative. The three issues were: first, duties and authorities of the military committee and the military commanding headquarter. Second, as soon as Tibet witnessed development in the spheres of politics, economics and culture, all regions of Tibet should be consolidated or united under a single administration. Third, Amdo should be included under the administrative jurisdiction of Tibet.

After much delay, the so-called the Dalai Lama's telegram to the PRC leadership, accepting the terms of the 17-Point Agreement, was sent on 24 October 1951. This telegram was shrouded in much controversy. The telegram was worded in typical communist language and it exhibited least similarity with the Dalai Lama's later works. Therefore, one cannot help doubting that the government of Tibet had submitted a draft telegraph to the Chinese representative and he had edited the telegraph as it was done to Ngabo's letter.

Had the Dalai Lama not returned to Lhasa from Dromo, the PRC might have implemented land reforms and demographic reforms policies in central Tibet right from 1951, like they had done in Kham and Amdo. In that case, central Tibet would have witnessed similar upheaval of social turmoil and mass hunger that the people of Kham and Amdo had to endure. These extreme policies when implemented in Kham and Amdo compelled the Tibetans there to escape to central Tibet en masse. Though catastrophic tragedies did befall on the people of the central Tibet eventually, starting from 1959, the Dalai Lama's return evidently delayed them and brought about eight years of relative peace and comfort.

Throughout history, until the Communist Chinese occupation in 1950, Tibet enjoyed independence. Even under the suzerainty of the Manchu Dynasty, the Tibetan Government conducted its own foreign affairs, maintained its own army, coined its own money, and exercised complete sovereignty in local affairs.

Meanwhile, the country's physical isolation, formerly its strongest protection from foreign interference in its affairs, overcome by the Communist Chinese through construction of a highway network from China to Tibet and within Tibet, and the establishment of plane service between Peking and Lhasa.

The conquest of Tibet and its integration with the Chinese mainland provides a highly illuminating study in contemporary Chinese politics. When the Communists took over Peking in 1949, Tibet was ruled by the youthful Dalai Lama, through a regent appointed to exercise control during his minority and a cabinet equally divided, between monks and nobles.

The population of Tibet within the de facto boundary was roughly about one and a half million persons. About one-third of the males were Buddhist monks. The Tibetan Army consisted of less than ten thousand troops with little modern equipment or training. Tibet's only real defence was its almost impenetrable terrain.

On September 2, 1949, the official Communist Chinese News Agency, NCNA, announced that Tibet must be "liberated," and that the Communist regime would not permit a "single inch of territory to remain outside the rule of the Chinese People's republic." But on the other hand on October 7, 1950, the Peking regime ordered the Communist Chinese army to march into Tibet. At the same time, it notified the Lhasa Government to send delegates to Peking "to conduct talk for the conclusion of an agreement on measures for the peaceful liberation of Tibet." Meantime on October 17, 1950, the invading Communist army crossed the Yangtze River into Tibet. At Chang-tu, in the Chamdo Area of Tibet, roughly 90 miles within the de facto boundary, the Tibetans made a vain effort to defend their country. "According to initial figures[37], 4000 men and officers were taken prisoner or killed by

---

[37] An NCNA dispatch dated November 2, 1950.

the People's Liberation Army…. Including more than twenty high ranking Tibetan officers and a high official whom Tibetan authorities had dispatched to Chang-tu."

Indian Government sent two protest notes to Peking expressing surprise that "military operations had been under-taken by the Chinese Government against peaceful people," and stating that the "invasion of Tibet cannot but be regarded as deplorable."

Peking answered the protest with amiable talk and immediately directed "the troops and work personnel entering Tibet" to undertake construction of two major arteries to link Tibet with China, the Sikang-Tibet and Tsinghai-Tibet highways.

In April 1951, a six-man delegation from Tibet arrived in Peking for negotiations with Communist Chinese Government. Kaloon Ngabou Ngawang Jigme, a noble, member of the Lhasa Cabinet and Governor of the Chamdo Area of Tibet, who was already in Peking, was designated head Tibetan delegate. The negotiations began on April 29, 1951. On May 23, 1951, the Communist-imposed peace treaty was signed.

Its important provisions, according to the text published by the Peking People's Daily, as follows:

1. That Tibet shall become a part of China. That the Government of Tibet "shall actively assist the Chinese People's Liberation Army to enter Tibet and consolidate the national Defence" of China.

2. That the Tibetan Army shall reorganize step by step into the Chinese Army and become a part of the national defence forces of China.

3. That the Chinese shall develop step by step the agriculture, industry, and commerce of Tibet.

4. That China shall have the handling of all external affairs of Tibet.

5. That China in order to ensure the implementation of this agreement shall set up a military and administrative committee and military area headquarters in Tibet.

The agreement further provided that 'the established status, functions, and powers of the Panchen shall be maintained. It specified that by this meant the status, functions and powers of the 13th Dalai and 9th Panchen Lama, when they were in friendly and amicable relations with each other.

China made certain promises in the treaty, which it has subsequently broken. That it would not alter:

1. The existing political system in Tibet.

2. The established status, functions, and power of the Dalai Lama.

3. The income of the monasteries.

In December 1952 the 1st local Congress of the Chinese Communist Party was held in Lhasa. Some 338 delegates attended, representing party members in the various units of the Tibetan Military Command. A dispatch[38] reported that the first Secretary Chang Kuo-hua reviewed the work carried out since the march into Tibet. Tibetan unit of Communist Chinese Army arbitrated the internal disputes of the Tibetans. With the help of the PLA troops, 14 primary schools with 1300 pupils have been opened, and over 400 Tibetan cadres have been trained. PLA units also distributed 18000 copies of the 'Agreement for the Peaceful Liberation of Tibet', and over 71000 copies of propaganda material in the Tibetan language. The Political

---

[38] An NCNA dispatch dated January 12, 1953.

Department of the Tibet Military District began publication of a semi-monthly paper called the 'Tibetan News'.

During 1953 the communist Chinese continued their cautious pace in Tibet with emphasis on indoctrination of the country's youth and attempts to win over high officials. However, work on the highways, was expedited. On the Sikang-Tibet highway work began eastward from Lhasa, as well as westward from Chang-tu.

The political development of 1954 was the summoning of the Dalai and Panchen to Peking. The Chinese created a third local political unit, Panchen Kampu Council at Shigatse to represent the Panchen. This not only cut the Dalai's power further, but also represented the small Shigatse area in the local affairs. On April 29, 1954, the Sino- Indian treaty, liquidating India's previous interests in Tibet was signed in Peking. The eight year pact recognizes by implication Chinese sovereignty in Tibet. It permits Indian trade agencies in the Tibetan border towns of Datung, Gyantse and Gartok, in return for Chinese trade agencies in India's two large cities, New Delhi and Calcutta, and in traditional trading centre at Kalimpong. It restricted pilgrim traffic between India and Lhasa, formerly heavy due to the many Indian Buddhists. All traders, pilgrims, and inhabitants of the Indo-Tibetan border area were required to carry passports and certification papers.

India also agreed to hand over to the Chinese at a reasonable price the postal, telegraph and telephone services and the rest houses formerly operated in Tibet by the Indian Government. This clause was carried out on April 1, 1955.

The Chinese Government summoned the Dalai and the Panchen to Peking, ostensibly to attend the 1st national Peoples' Congress. Both Grand Lamas were appointed deputies from Tibet. They departed in August and proceeded by separate routes to the Communist capital. Calcutta Statesman[39] reported that the Dalai's departure brought deep mourning in Tibet. The people threw themselves into the swollen Brahmaputra as their beloved leader crossed the river. Every-where they prostrated themselves before him, weeping. The devout saw an evil omen in the flood waters inundating their land.

The gods were displeased, but the caravan would go on. The Chinese mobilized their forces and from Chamdo they sent several thousand troops to act as escort to the youthful traveller. The Lamas arrived in Peking two weeks before the opening of the Congress. On September 16, the Dalai Lama summed up the difficulty of Tibetans in a speech before the congress with the statement that Communist China's army, including "working personnel and delegates of the Communist Government, have come to Tibet one after another and carried out Communist China's policy." The Dalai and Panchen were received by Mao Tse-tung. At the historic meeting Mao indicated that, among other impending charges, the Chinese intended to colonize Tibet at a ratio of more than five to one. This would make imposition of Chinese rule on Tibet much easier and at the same time would help solving China's chronic overpopulation problem, because Tibet was a large area but very thinly populated.

The Chinese plan for the complete reorganization of the Tibetan Government began to unfold early in 1955, with the adoption by the State Council of Communist china of the decision concerning the setting up of a preparatory Committee for the Tibetan Autonomous region. As an autonomous region, Tibet became a province of China. As stated by the Communist Chinese constitution it is an integral and

---

[39] Statesman (Daily News Paper), September 14, 1954, Calcutta.

inseparable part of the People's Republic of China under the leadership of the Central Government. An agreement was signed in Peking between the Tibetan Local Government and the Committee the Panchen Kanpo Lija on historical and unsettled problems. This established on paper the fact that the Dalai had been forced to give up an unhistorical portion of his power in local affairs to the Panchen and his followers.

Under the new setup the Government of Tibet remains actually under the Tibet military Command of the communist Chinese army. The powers of Tibet's former sovereign, the Dalai Lama, are severely curtailed. The Tibetan local government headed by the Dalai, had only 15 out of 51 seats on the new Committee.

The year 1956 had every indication of marking the end of the Tibet's history as a Buddhist theocracy. For the first time in the centuries of Tibet's existence, the life of Lamas and laymen was being dictated by a foreign government, ironically, one which subscribes to a philosophy, thoroughly alien to Buddhism, of atheistic materialism and expansion by force. The initial moves to force the Communist economic and social system on Tibet in defiance of the treaty agreement of 1951 were made in February 1956 on the country's eastern borders. The complete exploitation of the Tibetan economy through collectivization, was about to begin.

In June 1956, a group of Tibetans, headed by a brother of the Dalai Lama, addressed a petition to Indian Prime Minister Pt. Jawaharlal Nehru charging that the Communist Chinese killed more than 4000 Tibetans in the April bombing of the village of Litang, on the Chinese side of the Sino-Tibetan defacto boundary. The petition prepared at the birthplace of Buddha in India, and reported by news dispatched from Kalimpong, stated that liberation of Tibet was a deadly mockery. Indian Government had already cleared that India had no political or territorial ambitions in Tibet and did not seek any new or privileged position, but protested that the use of force "could not possibly be reconciled with a peaceful settlement." Possibility of outside instigation categorically denied.

In September 1956, Nepal and China signed a treaty in which Nepal recognized China's sovereignty over Tibet and surrenders the concessions it passed in Tibet under the treaty of 1856. But on the other hand Chou En Lai in December 1956, on his visit to India, assured Mr. Nehru that Tibet would enjoy autonomy and that China would not force communism on Tibet.

The Present Political Status of Tibet:

China's lack of trust in His Holiness the Dalai Lama and the Tibetan people is one of the most critical obstacles we currently face. The Chinese side is continuing to accuse His Holiness of pursuing some sort of "hidden agenda" because he has stated that he wants to look to the future instead of dwelling on the past in resolving the issue of Tibet. The Chinese side, however, insists that His Holiness the Dalai Lama make a public statement that Tibet has always been an integral part of China. This is a precondition for negotiations.

The Tibetan and Chinese sides have different viewpoints of their past relations. Our view in revisiting history will not serve any useful purpose. Debates over Tibet's history are counterproductive and will make it more difficult and complicated in resolving the issue. Our position is, therefore, to leave history aside and to focus on reaching a mutually acceptable solution for the future.

<u>Conflicting Views on the Current Situation Inside Tibet:</u>

Another major obstacle in Tibetan ongoing dialogue has been the conflicting perspectives on the current situation inside Tibet. The Chinese side insists that there are no problems in Tibet and that the "issue of Tibet" is only a creation of the Western anti-China forces. However, thousands of Tibetans from all corners of Tibet and from all walks of life, who manage to come out, tell a totally different story. They are nearly unanimous in reporting about the deep resentment and genuine grievances felt by Tibetans all over Tibet as a consequence of a rule that Tibetans experience as alien, colonial, chauvinistic and repressive. Against this background in order to have a common understanding of the real situation inside Tibet, Tibetans scholars proposed at the sixth meeting with Chinese counterparts that an opportunity to send study groups to look at the actual reality on the ground, in the spirit of "seeking truth from facts". This could help both sides to move beyond each other's contentions.

In 1979 Deng Xiaoping laid down the framework for resolving the issue of Tibet by stating that other than the issue of Tibetan independence anything else could be discussed and resolved. Consequently, His Holiness the Dalai Lama has repeatedly madeit clear that he is prepared to recognize today's reality that Tibet is a part of the People's Republic of China. The Middle Way Approach of His Holiness the Dalai Lama seeks to resolve the issue of Tibet within the framework of the PRC, while ensuring the full protection and survival of the Tibetan identity, culture, religion, and way of life.

<u>Restoring the integrity of Tibetan people:</u>

With this approach His Holiness the Dalai Lama has addressed the fundamental concern of the Chinese government by expressing his willingness to respect the sovereignty and territorial integrity of the People's Republic of China. As a response to His Holiness' courageous decision it is naturally Tibetan expectation that the Chinese leadership should reciprocate by acknowledging the legitimate needs of the Tibetan people.

Today, less than half of the Tibetan people reside in the so-called Tibet Autonomous Region. The rest lives in Tibetan autonomous counties and prefectures in Qinghai, Gansu, Sichuan and Yunnan provinces. All Tibetans in these areas share the same language, ethnicity, culture, and tradition. The Tibetan people yearn to be united in one administrative entity so that their way of life, tradition, language and religion can be preserved more effectively.

Historically the division of a nationality into many separate units contributed to the weakening and erosion of that nationality's unique identity and characteristics, as well as its ability to grow and develop.

The Chinese side argues that the present-day Tibet Autonomous Region parallels the territory under the former Tibetan government. As a result they reject Tibetan position as unreasonable. The Chinese viewpoint, however, will lead the discussions inevitably to the examination of Tibet's historical legal status under the Tibetan government before the so-called "peaceful liberation of Tibet" and will not help in reaching a common ground on which to build a common future.

The Chinese government has redrawn internal boundaries when it has suited its needs and could do so again in the case of Tibet.

Tibetans were not willing for the separation of these areas from China. More importantly, the Chinese government has already designated almost all of these areas as Tibet autonomous entities: the Tibet Autonomous Region, Tibet Autonomous Prefectures or Tibet Autonomous Counties. Thus, the Tibetan and Chinese views on what constitutes Tibet are really not so divergent.

The aspiration of the six million Tibetans to live in one single autonomous entity in a state of 1.3 billion people is neither an issue of creating a "greater" Tibet nor a cover for a separatist plot but a simple question of survival as a distinct people. In contrast it is rather a question of recognizing, restoring and respecting the integrity of the Tibetans as a distinct nationality within the PRC. Furthermore, this is not a new or revolutionary idea. From the beginning, when in 1951 the 17 Point Agreement was signed, successive Tibetan leaders have raised this issue and representatives of the Chinese government have recognized it as one that must be addressed.

Genuine Autonomy:

Some detractors in the Chinese Government allege that His Holiness' proposal for a single administrative entity for the Tibetan people and the implementation of genuine regional autonomy is really an effort to restore Tibet's former system of government, or to personally regain power over all of Tibet. Nothing is farther from the truth. In his March 10, 2005 statement His Holiness reiterated his position saying-

"My involvement in the affairs of Tibet is neither for the purpose of claiming certain personal rights or political position for myself nor attempting to stake claims for the Tibetan administration in exile. In 1992 in a formal announcement I stated clearly that when we return to Tibet with a certain degree of freedom I will not hold any office in the Tibetan government or any other political position and that the present Tibetan administration in exile will be dissolved. Moreover, the Tibetans working in Tibet should carry on the main responsibility of administering Tibet."

Benefits of Resolving the Tibet Issue Now:

Some detractors in the Chinese Government seem to believe that the aspirations of the Tibetan people will fizzle out once the Dalai Lama passes away. This is a most dangerous fallacy. Certainly, the absence of the Dalai Lama would be devastating for the Tibetan people. But the Tibetan freedom struggle will continue. The question is only whether this freedom struggle will continue remain strictly non-violent or not. It takes only a few desperate individuals or groups to create major instability in the volatile Central Asian region. This is not a threat, but a statement of a fact.

The Middle-Way Approach: A Framework for Resolving the Issue of Tibet:

The Middle-Way Approach is proposed by His Holiness the Dalai Lama to peacefully resolve the issue of Tibet and to bring about stability and co-existence between the Tibetan and Chinese people's based on equality and mutual co-operation. It is also a policy adopted democratically by the Central Tibetan Administration and the Tibetan people through a series of discussions held over a long time. This brief introduction to the Middle-Way policy and its history is intended for the Tibetan people inside and outside Tibet-and all those interested-to have a better understanding of the issues involved.

Tibetan people do not accept the present status of Tibet under the People's Republic of China. At the same time, they do not seek independence for Tibet, which is a historical fact. Treading a middle path in between these two lies the policy and means to achieve a genuine autonomy for all Tibetans, living in the three traditional provinces of Tibet within the framework of the People's Republic of China. This is called the Middle-Way Approach, a non-partisan and moderate position that safeguards the vital interests of all concerned parties-for Tibetans: the protection and preservation of their culture, religion and national identity; for the Chinese: the security and territorial integrity of the motherland; and for neighbours and other third parties: peaceful borders and international relations.

Although the 17-Point Agreement between the Tibetan government and the People's Republic of China was not reached on an equal footing or through mutual consent, His Holiness the Dalai Lama (just for the sake of the mutual benefit of the Tibetan and Chinese people's made all possible efforts to achieve a peaceful settlement with the Chinese government for eight years since 1951.) Even after His Holiness the Dalai Lama and the Kashag arrived in the Lokha region from Lhasa in 1959, he continued his efforts to achieve a negotiated settlement with the Chinese military officials. His attempts to abide by the terms of the 17-Point Agreement are analogous to the Middle-Way Approach. Unfortunately, the Chinese army unleashed a harsh military crackdown in Lhasa, Tibet's capital, and this convinced His Holiness the Dalai Lama that his hope for co-existence with the Chinese government was no longer possible. Under the circumstances, he had no other option but to seek refuge in India and work in exile for the freedom and happiness of all the Tibetan people.

Soon after his arrival in Tezpur, India, His Holiness the Dalai Lama issued a statement on 18 April 1959, explaining that the 17-Point Agreement was signed under duress and that the Chinese government had deliberately violated the terms of the Agreement. Thus from that day onwards, he declared that the agreement would be considered null and void, and he would strive for the restoration of Tibet's independence. Since then until 1979, the Central Tibetan Administration and the Tibetan people adopted a policy of seeking independence for Tibet. However, the world in general has become increasingly interdependent politically, militarily and economically and as a result great changes have been taking place in the independent status of countries and nationalities. In China also, changes will certainly take place and a time will come for both sides to engage in actual negotiations. Therefore, His Holiness the Dalai Lama has believed for a long time that in order to resolve the Tibetan issue through negotiations, it is more beneficial to change the policy of restoring Tibetan independence to an approach that offers mutual benefits to China as well as to Tibet.

Although this approach occurred to His Holiness the Dalai Lama a long time ago, he did not decide it arbitrarily or thrust it upon others. Since the early 1970s, he held a series of discussions on this issue with, and solicited suggestions from, the Chairperson and Vice-Chairperson of the Assembly of Tibetan People's Deputies, the Kashag and many scholarly and experienced people. Particularly in 1979, the late Chinese paramount leader, Deng Xiaoping's proposal to His Holiness the Dalai Lama that "except independence, all other issues can be resolved through negotiations", was very much in agreement with His Holiness the Dalai Lama's long-held belief of finding a mutually-beneficial solution. Immediately, His Holiness the Dalai Lama gave a favourable response by agreeing to undertake negotiations and decided to change the policy of restoring Tibet's independence to that of the Middle-Way Approach. This decision was again taken after a due process of consultations with the then Assembly of Tibetan People's Deputies, the Kashag and many scholarly and experienced people. Therefore, this Approach is not something that has emerged all of a sudden; it has a definite history of evolution.

The Middle-Way Approach was Adopted Democratically:

Since the decision to pursue the Middle-Way Approach and before His Holiness the Dalai Lama issued a statement in the European parliament in Strasbourg on 15 June 1988 which formed the basis of our negotiations as to what kind of autonomy was needed by the Tibetan people a four day special conference was organised in Dharamsala from 6 June 1988. This conference was attended by the members of the Assembly of Tibetan People's Deputies and the Kashag, public servants, all the Tibetan settlement officers and the members of the local Tibetan Assemblies, representatives from the Tibetan NGOs, newly-arrived Tibetans and special invitees. They held extensive discussions on the text of the proposal and finally endorsed it unanimously.

Since the Chinese government did not respond positively to the proposal, His Holiness the Dalai Lama again proposed in 1996 and 1997 that the Tibetan people should decide on the best possible way of realizing the cause of Tibet through a referendum. Accordingly, a preliminary opinion poll was conducted in which more than 64% of the total opinion letters received expressed that there was no need to hold a referendum, and that they would support the Middle-Way Approach, or whatever decisions His Holiness the Dalai Lama takes from time to time, in accordance with the changing political situation in China and the world at large. To this effect, the Assembly of Tibetan People's Deputies adopted a unanimous resolution on 18 September 1997 and informed His Holiness the Dalai Lama. Responding to this, His Holiness the Dalai Lama said in his 10th March statement of 1998:

> "Last year, we conducted an opinion poll of the Tibetans in exile and collected suggestions from Tibet wherever possible on the proposed referendum, by which the Tibetan people were to determine the future course of our freedom struggle to their full satisfaction. Based on the outcome of this poll and suggestions from Tibet, the Assembly of Tibetan People's Deputies, our parliament in exile, passed a resolution empowering me to continue to use my discretion on the matter without seeking recourse to a referendum. I wish to thank the people of Tibet for the tremendous trust, confidence and hope they place in me. I continue to believe that my Middle-Way Approach is the most realistic and pragmatic course to resolve the issue of Tibet peacefully. This approach meets the vital needs of the Tibetan people while ensuring the unity and stability of the People's Republic of China. I will, therefore, continue to pursue this course of approach with full commitment and make earnest efforts to reach out to the Chinese leadership"

This policy was, hence, adopted taking into account the opinion of the Tibetan people and a unanimous resolution passed by the Assembly of Tibetan People's Deputies.

Important Components of the Middle-Way Approach:

1. Without seeking independence for Tibet, the Central Tibetan Administration strives for the creation of a political entity comprising the three traditional provinces of Tibet.

2. Such an entity should enjoy a status of genuine national regional autonomy.

3. This autonomy should be governed by the popularly-elected legislature and executive through a democratic process and should have an independent judicial system.

4. As soon as the above status is agreed upon by the Chinese government, Tibet would not seek separation from, and remain within, the People's Republic of China.

5. Until the time Tibet is transformed into a zone of peace and non-violence, the Chinese government can keep a limited number of armed forces in Tibet for its protection.

6. The Central Government of the People's Republic of China has the responsibility for the political aspects of Tibet's international relations and defense, whereas the Tibetan people should manage all other affairs pertaining to Tibet, such as religion and culture, education, economy, health, ecological and environmental protection.

7. The Chinese government should stop its policy of human rights violations in Tibet and the deliberate emigration of Chinese population into Tibetan areas.

8. To resolve the issue of Tibet, His Holiness the Dalai Lama shall take the main responsibility of sincerely pursuing negotiations and reconciliation with the Chinese government.

Considering the fact that the unity and co-existence between the Tibetan and Chinese people is more important than the political requirements of the Tibetan people, His Holiness the Dalai Lama has pursued a mutually-beneficial Middle-Way policy, which is a great political step forward. Irrespective of population size, economy or military strength, the equality of nationalities means that all nationalities can co-exist on an equal footing, without any discrimination based on one nationality being superior or better than the other. As such, it is an indispensable criterion for ensuring unity among the nationalities. If the Tibetan and Chinese peoples can co-exist on an equal footing, this will serve as the basis for guaranteeing the unity of nationalities, social stability and territorial integrity of the People's Republic of China, which are of paramount importance to China. Therefore, the special characteristic of the Middle-Way Approach is that it can achieve peace through non-violence, mutual benefit, unity of nationalities and social stability.

<u>Tibet Seeks the Moral Stand for Freedom of the World and Democracy:</u>

Freedom of expression and transparency are essential parts of a healthy democracy. In China and Tibet people cannot exercise their right to vote effectively or take part in public decision-making if they do not have free access to information and ideas and are not able to express their views freely.

Since the 1970s there has been a steady progress toward democracy and rule by the people. Authoritarian regimes and military dictatorships have fallen and communism collapsed throughout the Soviet bloc. In most cases, these systems have given way to electoral democracy and constitutional government. Major exceptions remain, but today electoral democracy is practised in more than 130 out of 193 countries in the world.

Freedom of information, speech and the press is firmly rooted in the structures of modern democratic thought. With limited restrictions, every democracy has legal provisions protecting these rights.

The UN Declaration of Human Rights, adopted by the general assembly in 1948 declares "Everyone has the right to freedom of opinion and expression; this right includes freedom to hold opinions without interference and to seek, receive and impart information and ideas through any media and regardless of frontiers" (although as Article 19, it comes after the right to hold property, be married and hold a nationality, among others).

As such, morals and ethics heavily favour the nearly unfettered rights to speech, press and information. While rights might be tailored to protect state security from a Lockesian social contract perspective, a Kantian categorical outlook surely provides for a society in which everyone can speak freely.

Freedom of speech is thus not only essential for individual dignity but also to participation, accountability and democracy. Violations of freedom of expression often go hand in hand with other violations, in particular the right to freedom of association and assembly. However one, particular form of expression which is banned in some countries is considered as "hate speech" because some views might incite intolerance or hatred.

Communism, primarily as an economic system, is much quieter on the issue of individual human rights and dignity in recent decades. Two conflicting positions on these freedoms arise with a self-centred attitude. The first is an argument against individual freedoms. In a communist society, the individual's best interests are indistinguishable from the society's best interest. Thus, the idea of individual freedom is silenced in a communist ideology on the pretext of pro-poor collectivism.

The only reason to hold individual speech and information rights must be to praise the party, a condition which would likely be met only in certain instances rather than across time, but it will gradually be viewed as an infringement on freedom , dignity and human rights.

On the other hand, the idea of perfect equality in official documents argues for a right of expression and press. Since each individual is equally important, each should have an equally valid point of view. Indeed, Marx defended the right to a freedom of the press, arguing in 1842 that restrictions, like censorship were instituted by the bourgeois elite. He claimed censorship is a tool of the powerful to oppress the powerless. That is what the world is seeing in Tibet and in recent events in Hong Kong.

Many implementations of communism favoured a constitutional democracy, albeit usually with only one party. Before and at the creation of many communist countries, a desire for freedom from the oppression of the proletariat by the bourgeois translated into strongly voiced support for individual freedoms for speech, dissent and information.

By encouraging China to prepare for wars before he took power over China, Chairman Mao, proclaimed

"The people should subject ... the party in power, to severe criticism, and press and impel it to give up its one-party, one-class dictatorship and act according to the opinions of the people....The second matter concerns freedom of speech, assembly and association for the people. Without freedom, it will be impossible to carry out the democratic reconstruction of the political system."

Thus, on the balance, it seems communist theory is compatible with freedoms of speech, information and protest, but it is far from a basic freedoms and rights such as it is under democracy and individual-centred systems like that of Kant and Locke. Freedom of information should only be granted when the party as a whole is likely to benefit.

In this light, it is unrealistic that communist leaders, while still a persecuted opposition philosophy, would strongly support speech rights and later reject them when communism becomes the ruling system. At that point, access to oppositional speech and information is no longer beneficial to the communist regime, and thus is no longer workable in a single party system.

Today China, more than almost any other country in the world, severely restricts its own citizens' freedom of expression and human rights. Oddly enough, Article 35 of the current Chinese constitution, written in 1982, stipulates "Citizens of the PRC have freedom of speech, publication, assembly, association, procession and demonstration."

That the abovementioned hardline policy of China and the abusive rhetoric accompanying it, has failed and disastrously so was made amply clear by the recent month-long demonstrations in Tibet. The top Chinese leaders have been informed that this hardline policy is wrong by no less a figure than Baba Phuntsok Wangyal, the founder of the Tibetan Communist Party, who played a key role in cementing Chinese Communist rule in Tibet. In his letter of 29 October 2004 addressed to President Hu Jintao, he said:

"As far as how to solve the Tibetan issue is concerned, since the fundamental nature of the question is absolutely related with domestic matters, so under the premise regarding the sovereignty of the nation it is merely a demand for meaningful autonomy and slight changes in the administrative division policy. In addition, as to the essence and preconditions of this matter, every one of us can and should reach a common understanding. With this as a base, and after the Central Government and the Dalai Lama have reached a mutual understanding on the principles regarding national sovereignty, appropriate adjustments to the domestic administrative division policy and implementing the right to self-determination, both sides should officially declare in a political statement that friendly relations between them have been restored. Within such a friendly and harmonious environment, regarding the concrete formations, plans, and schedules for unifying the Tibetan autonomous regions- including temporarily establishing a transitional consultative department in order to assure the united autonomy of its fundamental content and destination being achieved - both sides should be strategic, far-sighted and generous, adhering to the brotherly relationship."

Wang Lixiong, a Beijing-based writer, reinforces Phuntsok Wangyal's argument. On 28 March 2008 his op-ed piece appeared on The Wall Street Journal. In this piece he says that China's current anti-splittism struggle is wrong. He says:

"Having invested their careers in anti-splittism, these people cannot admit the idea is mistaken without losing face and, they fear, losing their own power and position as well."

"The most efficient route to peace in Tibet is through the Dalai Lama, whose return to Tibet would immediately alleviate a number of problems. Much of the current ill will, after all, is the direct result of the Chinese government's verbal attacks on the Dalai Lama, who, for Tibetan monks, has an incomparably lofty status. To demand that monks denounce him is about as practical asking that they vilify their own parents."

Wang Lixiong initiated the recent 12-point statement on Tibet with 30 Chinese intellectuals. In fact, since the statement was first issued, many more Chinese human rights and environmental activists, writers and scholars have signed up. The first point says. "At present the one-sided propaganda of the official Chinese media is having the effect of stirring up inter-ethnic animosity and aggravating an already tense situation. This is extremely detrimental to the long-term goal of safeguarding national unity. We call for this to be stopped."

The second point says, "We support the Dalai Lama's appeal for peace and hope that the ethnic conflict can be dealt with according to the principles of goodwill, peace and non-violence. We condemn any violent act against innocent people, strongly urge the Chinese government to stop the violent suppression and appeal to the Tibetan people likewise not to engage in violent activities." The statement urges the Chinese government to hold direct talks with His Holiness the Dalai Lama to resolve the issue.

Ruan Ming, a speechwriter for former CCP General Secretary Hu Yaobang, has a different take on the tense situation in Tibet. Ruan Ming who lives in Taiwan told The Epoch Times on 26 March that "The Dalai Lama has always proposed a peaceful solution to Tibetan issues and won the world's recognition. With that in mind, the CCP has framed the Dalai Lama for having 'carefully planned and stirred up the event.'" Ruan Ming added, "This is exactly how the CCP framed Zhao Ziyang for the Tiananmen Massacre in 1989 and accused Zhao of 'splitting the Party and supporting unrest.'" Ruan Ming added, "The Dalai Lama already said he would resign if the unrest continued. The Dalai Lama is influential globally and if he really retired, the CCP could greatly push and label the Tibetans as terrorists like the Xinjiang independence movement. This will give the CCP an excuse to ignore Tibetan appeals and further repress them."

On 27 March 2008, more than 70 Tibetologists sent an open letter to President Hu Jintao. In this letter, the scholars said, "As scholars engaged in Tibetan Studies, we are especially disturbed by what has been happening. The civilization we study is not simply a subject of academic enquiry; it is the heritage of a living people and one of the world's great cultural legacies…The attribution of the current unrest to the Dalai Lama represents a reluctance on the part of the Chinese government to acknowledge and engage with policy failures that are surely the true cause of popular discontent."

<u>**Indian Leaders on Tibetan Issue:**</u>

C. Rajagopalachari's[40] view was that it is brutal Colonialism is in Tibet:

"The issue of Tibet is not a question of legalistic exploration as to the sovereignty of Tibet but a question of human rights, which must be decided on the plane of justice and humanity and not on the basis of any legal puzzle.

"His Holiness the Dalai Lama in his message had made thing quite clear and pointed out how even on a legalistic plain there can be no doubt about the rights of the Tibetan people to rule themselves irrespective of any belonging to other nationalities. This invasion of Tibet, which resulted in His Holiness taking refuge in Indian Territory, is brutal colonialism. There can, therefore, be no second thoughts in the matter. All Indian people want Tibet to be released from the grip of China."

Dr. Rajendra Prasad:[41]

"Freedom is the most sacred boon. It has to be protected by all means, violent or non-violent. Therefore, Tibet has to be liberated from the iron grip of China and handed over to the Tibetans."

"The Chinese invaders have plundered Tibet and destroyed its peaceful citizens. Tibet is nearer to India in religion and culture. We have to, therefore, try hard to rescue Tibet from the bloody clutches of the plunderer and let its people breathe in free air. If China stealthily infiltrates our land, they should be ruthlessly turned back."

---

[40] C. Rajagopalachari, the last Governor-General of India, on Tibet.
[41] Dr. Rajendra Prasad, the first President of Indian Republic, on Tibet, Excerpts from his last public speech, Gandhi Maidan, Patna, 24 October, 1962.

"The world stands witness to the fact that India has never cast a vicious glance on any country. But in war, we have to give a fight at any place or land convenient to us in facing enemy."

"When we were raising slogan of '*Hindi-Chini, Bhai-Bhai*', China was busy nibbling our land and through brute betrayal captured about 12 thousand square miles of our land. It is imperative that like a disciplined nation, we should face the invaders. There is no doubt that we will clear our motherland of these invaders."

Pt. Jawaharlal Nehru:[42]

"Since Tibet is not the same as China, it should ultimately be the wishes of the people of Tibet that should prevail and not any legal or constitutional arguments. That, I think, is a valid point."

"I can see no difficulty in saying to the Chinese Government that whether they have suzerainty or sovereignty over Tibet, surely, according to any principles, principles they proclaim and the principles I uphold, the last voice in regard to Tibet should be the voice of the people of Tibet and of nobody else."

"When Prime Minister of China Chou En Lai came to India two or three years ago, he was good enough to discuss Tibet with me[43] at considerable length. We had a frank and full talk. He told me that while Tibet had long been a part of China, they did not consider Tibet as a province of China. The people are different from the people of China

---

[42] The first Prime Minister of India, on Tibet Address to the Lok Sabha, 7 December, 1950.
[43] Pt. Jawaharlal Nehru: Statement to the Lok Sabha, 27 April, 1959.

proper. Therefore, they considered Tibet as an autonomous region, which could enjoy autonomy. He told me further that it was absurd for anyone to imagine that China was going to force communism on Tibet."

Sardar Vallabhbhai Patel:[44]

"The Chinese Government has tried to delude us by professions of peaceful intentions. My own feeling is that at a crucial period they managed to instil into our ambassador a false sense of confidence in their so-called desire to settle the Tibetan problem by peaceful means."

"The final action of the Chinese, in my judgment, is little short of perfidy. The tragedy of it is that the Tibetans put faith in us; they choose to be guided by us; and we have been unable to get them out of the meshes of Chinese diplomacy or Chinese malevolence. From the latest position, it appears that we shall not be able to rescue the Dalai Lama."

"It is impossible to imagine any sensible person believing in the so-called threat to China from Anglo-American machinations in Tibet. During the last several months, outside the Russian camp, we have practically been alone in championing the cause of Chinese entry into the UN and in securing from the Americans assurances on the question of Formosa. I doubt if we can go any further than we have done already to convince China of our good intentions, friendliness and goodwill. Their last telegram to us is an act of gross discourtesy not only in the summary way it disposes of our protest against the entry of Chinese

---

[44] Sardar Vallabhbhai Patel, the first Deputy Prime Minister of India, on Tibet 07 November, 1950. New Delhi.

forces into Tibet but also in the wild insinuation that our attitude is determined by foreign influences. It looks as though it is not a friend speaking in that language but a potential enemy."

"We have to consider what new situation now faces us as a result of the disappearance of Tibet, as we knew, it and the expansion of China almost up to our gates. Throughout history we have seldom been worried about our northeast frontier. The Himalayas have been regarded as an impenetrable barrier against any threat from the north. We had a friendly Tibet, which gave us no trouble."

"We seem to have regarded Tibetan autonomy as extending independent treaty relationship. The undefined state of the frontier and the existence on our side of the population with its affinities to Tibetans or Chinese have all the elements of potential trouble between China and ourselves."

"Chinese ambitions in this respect not only cover the Himalayan slopes on our side but also include important parts of Assam. They have their ambitions in Burma also. Burma has the added difficulty that it has no McMahon Line round which to build up even the semblance of an agreement. Our northern or north-eastern approaches consist of Nepal, Bhutan, and Sikkim, the Darjeeling area and tribal areas in Assam. From the point of view of communications, they are weak spots. Continuous defensive lines do not exist. There is almost an unlimited scope for infiltration."

"In my judgment, the situation is one in which we cannot afford either to be complacent or to be vacillating. We must have a clear idea of what we wish to achieve and also of the methods by which we should achieve it."

"It is, of course, impossible for me to be exhaustive in setting out all these problems. I am, however, giving below some of the problems which, in my opinion, require early solution and around which we have to build our administrative or military policies and measures to implement them."

1. Military and intelligence appreciation of the Chinese threat to India both on the frontier and to internal security.

2. An examination of our military position.

3. An appraisement of the strength of our forces.

4. A long-term consideration of our defence needs.

5. The question of Chinese entry into UN.

6. The political and administrative steps which we should take to strengthen our northern and north-eastern frontiers.

7. Measures of internal security in the border areas well as the States flanking those areas, such as U.P., Bihar, Bengal and Assam.

8. Improvement of our communications, road, rail, air and wireless, in these areas and with the frontier outposts.

9. The future of our mission at Lhasa and the trade posts at Gyangtse and Yatung and the forces which we have in operation in Tibet to guard the trade routes.

10. The policy in regard to the McMahon Line.

CHAPTER III

TIBETAN POLICY OF CHINA

China's Tibetan policy has not been consistent as it was influenced either by hardliners or moderates at different times. The domestic policies of China and the external environment equally impacted its Tibet policy. In the early 50s, China did not face much international hostility in the matter of the occupation of Tibet when the PLA marched into Tibet since the USA was deeply involved in Korean War and the Taiwan Strait crisis and the nations of the world were re-grouping themselves in the frame of the ensuing Cold War. There are five discernible phases of different approaches in China's Tibet policy:

1. **Phase I from 1951 to 1959:**

The 1951 agreement, if we look back, grants full autonomy to Tibet in the matters of governance, religion, language and culture and of preserving the traditional religious and administrative institutions like the institutions of the Dalai Lama and Panchen Lama within the geographical boundaries of Tibet while vesting the foreign and defence matters with the Chinese central government. However, as a young communist nation, China was in great hurry to introduce communist reforms in Tibet. It was a sudden and painful experience for Tibetans who had been leading an almost isolated and different system for several centuries, away from external interference. Tibet was neutral during the World War II. This alienated the Tibetan people and their leadership. As a result riots and rebellion broke out in Tibet many times between

1952 and 1957, with certain external support. Mao in Feb 1957 had said that conditions in Tibet were not ripe for reforms and that the implementation of reforms be postponed till 1962. He also offered to reduce the Han cadres in Tibet. The Dalai Lama had dismissed two Prime Ministers who insulted the Chinese in early 1950s. Mao's policy of moderation and gradualism also had the support of the Dalai Lama and the Tibetan elite but it was not implemented in practice. The flight of the Dalai Lama and his supporters to India in 1959 marks the end this phase.

2. Phase II from 1959 to 1976:

This is the critical period of Chinese handling of Tibet issue. It was dominated by the hard line policies and internal power struggle in China. The 'Great Leap Forward' and 'Great Proletarian Cultural Revolution' brought unparallel disorder within China. The excesses by the CPC members in Tibet like attack on religious institutions, culture and language and increasingly strained relationship with India only further alienated the Tibetans. China reorganized Tibet by making U-tsang as Tibet Autonomous Region and merging Kham and Amdo regions with Yunnan, Sichuan, Gansu and Qinghai provinces.

3. Phase III from 1978 to 1986:

This is the period when Deng Xiaoping adopted soft policy to handle Tibet issue and for the first time proposed talks with the Dalai Lama. This policy also ended in failure but a communication line was set up for the first time between the Dalai Lama and the Chinese leadership.

4. **Phase IV from 1987 to 2001:**

The failure of Deng's soft policy emboldened the hands of the hawks in the CPC and China adopted a different approach to solve the Tibet issue through economic development instead of focusing on political solution alone. This model has met with partial success as the Dalai Lama diluted his demand from independence to autonomy, yet the Chinese leadership did not show much interest in carrying any negotiations with the Tibetan leadership.

5. **Phase V 2002 onwards:**

This period is marked by realistic handling of the Tibetan issue, which combines winning the people of Tibet through economic development and conducting dialogue with the Tibetan leadership in exile.

A good number of international Tibetan historians and Tibetologists have done a great deal of research on the matter to the extent that there seems to be no area left for further research. But curious minds wonder what made the Dalai Lama and his government chose to return to Lhasa from Dromo, after Ngabo signed the 17-Point Agreement[45] without the consent of the Dalai Lama and the Kashag (the cabinet of the government of Tibet). In fact the Dalai Lama and his government could have renounced it out right, and possibly escaped from Tibet. Why did not the Dalai Lama disown the agreement when America was determined to help Tibet? The US wanted the Dalai Lama to clearly reject the agreement and resist Chinese invasion.

---

[45] Marie & Buffetrille edited, Authenticating *Tibet* 2008, p. 68.

As soon as the PRC was founded on 1st October 1949, the government of China pronounced their intention of incorporating Tibet into China in no uncertain language. The Tibetan programme of Peking radio and Siling (Xining) radio repeatedly blared that the PLA would be dispatched to Tibet to "liberate" it from foreign imperialists.[46] At the same time Lhalu, the then Governor-General of Chamdo, telegrammed the Kashag that the Communist Chinese were camping to the east of Chamdo in large numbers and there was a possible danger of Chinese invasion.[47]

The status of Tibet is at the core of the dispute, as it has been for all parties drawn into it over the past century. China maintains that Tibet is an inalienable part of China. Tibetans maintain that Tibet has historically been an independent country. In reality, the conflict over Tibet's status has been a conflict over history. When Chinese writers and political figures assert that Tibet is a part of China, they do so not on the basis of Chinese rule being good rule (although they do not hesitate to make that assertion), but on the basis of history.

The fundamental place of history in the Tibet issue is not something imposed by outside parties. Even though the Dalai Lama and his government-in-exile appear quite at ease with accepting Tibet as a part of China, the People's Republic of China (PRC) has pointedly accused the Dalai Lama of duplicity, stating that his unwillingness to recognize Tibet as having been an integral part of China for centuries renders his acquiescence unacceptable. The centrality of history in the question of Tibet's status could not be clearer.

---

[46] Shakapa 1976 Vol. II, [Tibetan] p. 408.
[47] 14th Dalai Lama, *My Land and My People,* 1962, p. 88.

The evolution of both Chinese and Tibetan positions, then at the prevailing views currently held by advocates on either side of the issue, and finally at how the major assertions made about Tibet's historical status stand up against the historical record as reflected in relevant primary-source materials in Chinese and Tibetan. Contemporary secondary literature on the Tibet issue has until now not been based on this sort of approach.

New details and new insights are crucial for those concerned with the basic historical arguments that underlie the crucial issue of Tibet's status. It will show that positions on the Tibet issue said to be reflective of centuries of popular consensus, are actually very recent constructions often at variance with the history on which they claim to be based. In some areas critical aspects of history have been misconstrued by both sides.

Thus, China's contention that Tibet has been an "integral" part of China since the thirteenth century took shape only in the twentieth century. Moreover, as late as the 1950s, Chinese writers were accustomed to describing Tibet's place in the world of imperial China as that of a subordinate vassal state, not an integral part of China, as current Chinese materials put it. Indeed, for quite some time after Tibet was incorporated into the PRC, Chinese narratives of that process were often vague and beset by contradictory chronologies.

Similarly, the Tibetan concept of a "priest-patron" religious relationship governing Sino-Tibetan relations to the exclusion of concrete political subordination is itself a rather recent construction. Ample evidence is there to show that Tibetan religious figures entertained religious and spiritual relationships with emperors of several dynasties, sometimes under conditions in which Tibet was politically subordinate to the dynasty in question and at other times under conditions in which Tibet was independent. The priest-patron relationship was simply not a barometer of Tibet's status, in spite of current Tibetan use of it as such.

In addition, one of the major contentions of the Tibetan government-in-exile, that Tibet was invaded in 1949, is a complex and ambiguous issue. The Tibetan government signalled it was under attack only in 1950, when PRC forces crossed into the territories under the jurisdiction of the Dalai Lama's government. Tibetan areas outside the Dalai Lama's jurisdiction had already been incorporated into the PRC. The insistence in recent decades on 1949 as the date of Tibet's invasion is an attempt to define these territories as part of Tibet. Complexity is added to the issue by the fact that these territories have been significant in Tibet's conflict with China. Their cultural place in the Tibetan world is important; the present Dalai Lama comes from this part of the Tibetan Plateau.

<u>Tibet's Traditional Society and Democracy in Exile:</u>

The 13th Dalai Lama had abolished the system of demanding free transport from the local land-holding peasants by officials travelling on duty and had fixed charges for the use of horses, mules and yaks. The 14th Dalai Lama went one step further and ordered that in future no transport service should be demanded without the special sanction of the government. He also increased the rates to be paid for transport services.

Foreigners like Charles Bell, Hugh Richardson, and Heinrich Harrier, who lived and worked in independent Tibet, were impressed by the average standard of living of ordinary Tibetans, which they said was higher than in many Asian countries.

Famine and starvation were unheard of in Tibet until after the Chinese invasion. There were, of course, years of poor harvests and crop failures. But people could easily borrow from the buffer stock held by the district administrations, monasteries, aristocrats and rich farmers.

When the 14th Dalai Lama assumed the throne, he constituted a reform committee to introduce fundamental land reforms, but the Chinese communists, fearing that these would take the wind out of their sails, prevented His Holiness the Dalai Lama from carrying out his proposed reforms. In his autobiography, 'My Land and My People', His Holiness the Dalai Lama writes,

> "I managed to make some fundamental reforms. I appointed a Reforms Committee of fifty members, lay and monk officials and representatives of the monasteries, and a smaller standing committee to examine all the reforms that were needed and report to the larger body, and thence to me."

In 1959, after his flight to freedom, His Holiness the Dalai Lama re-established his government in India and initiated a series of democratic reforms. A popularly-elected body of people's representatives, the parliament-in-exile, was constituted. In 1963 a detailed draft constitution for future Tibet was promulgated. Despite strong opposition, the Dalai Lama insisted on the inclusion of a clause empowering the Tibetan parliament to revoke his executive powers by a majority of two-thirds of its total members in consultation with the Supreme Court, if this was seen to be in the highest interest of the nation.

In 1990 further democratic changes were introduced by increasing the strength of the Assembly of Tibetan People's Deputies (ATPD) the defacto parliament from 12 to 46. It was given more constitutional powers such as the election of Kalons (ministers), who were previously appointed directly by the Dalai Lama. The Supreme Justice Commission was set up to look into people's grievances against the Administration.

In 2001 the Tibetan parliament, on the advice of His Holiness the Dalai Lama, amended the exile Tibetan constitution to provide for the direct election of the Kalon Tripa (the chairman of the Cabinet or Kashag) by the exile population. Since the establishment of the new system the Tibetan exiles have elected the Kalon Tripa twice.

Years in exile have also seen the growth of a strong and vibrant Tibetan civil society with its own distinct voice and vision. The emergence of NGOs like the Tibetan Youth Congress, the Tibetan Women's Association, the Tibetan National Democratic Party, the Tibetan Centre for Human Rights and Democracy and many others in the fields of education, health, culture and environment, which have strengthened the roots of democracy in exile and have also served as a forum for the training of future leaders. The degree of the openness of the exile Tibetan community is reflected by the fact that in the late 1970's a Tibetan Communist Party appeared on the exile Tibetan scene.

Looking to future Tibet, in February 1992 the Dalai Lama announced the Guidelines for Future Tibet's Polity and the Basic Features of its Constitution, wherein he stated that he would not "play any role in the future government of Tibet, let alone seek the Dalai Lama's traditional political position". The future government of Tibet, the Dalai Lama said, would be elected by the people on the basis of adult franchise.

In a statement on 10th March 2003, His Holiness the Dalai Lama said:

"It is necessary to recognize that the Tibetan freedom struggle is not about my personal position or well-being. As early as 1969 I made it clear that it is up to the Tibetan people to decide whether the centuries-old institution of the Dalai Lama should continue or not. In 1992 in a formal announcement I stated clearly that when we return to Tibet with a certain degree of freedom I would not hold any office in the Tibetan government or any other political position. However, as I often state, till my last day I will remain committed to the promotion of human values and religious harmony. I also announced then that the Tibetan Administration-in-Exile should be dissolved and that the Tibetans in Tibet must shoulder the main responsibility of running the Tibetan government. I have always believed that in the future Tibet should follow a secular and democratic system of governance. It is, therefore, baseless to allege that our efforts are aimed at the restoration of Tibet's old social system. No Tibetan, whether in exile or in Tibet, has any desire to restore old Tibet's outdated social order. On the contrary, the democratization of the Tibetan community started soon upon our arrival in exile. This culminated in the direct election of our political leadership in 2001. We are committed to continue to take vigorous actions to further promote democratic values among the ordinary Tibetans."

Present Situation of Human Rights in Tibet:

The Human Rights situation of minority nationalities, including Tibetan has become a major issue in the People's Republic of China (PRC). Although the Constitution of the PRC guarantees its citizen freedom of speech, press, assembly, association, demonstration and religious belief, the double standard in its implementation has become a glaring reality.

Tibetans' petitions, street protests, peaceful assembly and demonstrations against the denial of their fundamental rights bring more arrests, prison sentences and torture in Tibet. Arbitrary detention, sentencing, disappearances, interrogation and torture of Tibetans have become a common practice. As a result, Tibetans of all ages and all walks of life across the Tibetan plateau have resisted through the tragic acts of self-immolation protests in the last few years.

Since the 10th of March 2008, a series of massive demonstrations rocked all over Tibet. Beijing made several allegations. Beijing accused the Dalai clique of masterminding" these demonstrations. Beijing said these demonstrations were violent and organised by terrorists, and these demonstrations were aimed at splitting Tibet from the motherland. Premier Wen Jiabao told the international media on 18 March 2008 that his government had ample facts and plenty of evidence to prove that the recent riot in Lhasa was organised, premeditated, masterminded and incited by the Dalai Lama clique.

Official China claims that these demonstrations prove that His Holiness the Dalai Lama's advocacy of non-violence is just a lip service. China says that Dharamsala has become the epicentre of lies and the government-in-exile has churned out groundless fabrication since the riot in Lhasa.

China claims that the appeals issued by His Holiness the Dalai Lama to our Chinese brothers and sisters are his attempt to stir up more unrest in Tibet. The Chinese authorities said that the Dalai Clique's statements also attempted to stir up hostility between ethnic groups in Tibet and internationalize the so-called Tibet issue.

In fact the war of words is so intense from the Chinese side that they have already published a book called *Lies and Truth*. The lies are all on the Tibetan side and the truth is with Beijing. The book was launched on 4 April in Beijing by Sanlian, a unit of the China Publishing Group. The publishers claim the publication of Lies and Truth is the fastest ever in publishing history. The book was commissioned on 27 March and published on 3 April. The publisher of Sanlian, Zhang Weimin told China's CCTV that "We had to frame a response to demonstrate our position. We worked to show the true state of things to those unaware of the truth, and to rebut the axe-grinding, misleading reports of the western media."

The book consists of previously published articles. It regurgitates all the official allegations of Beijing that the "Dalai clique" is behind the current unrest in Tibet. Lies and Truth is an attempt to refute "the distortions" of the western media in its reporting of the current problems in Tibet. The book contains a large section in which all the "major achievements in economic, cultural and social development" in Tibet are explained.

Ultimately Lies and Truth is aimed at the Chinese people. The sweep of the western media and the breadth of its coverage of China's Tibet headache have shaken the Chinese people's faith in their own government and its handling of the Tibet issue. This has forced Beijing to make an attempt, however thin, to explain its actions and policies to its own people.

The term TIBET here means the whole of Tibet known as Cholka-Sum (U-Tsang, Kham and Amdo). It includes the present-day Chinese administrative areas of the so-called Tibet Autonomous Region, Qinghai Province, two Tibetan Autonomous Prefectures and one Tibetan Autonomous County in Sichuan Province, one Tibetan

Autonomous Prefecture and one Tibetan Autonomous County in Gansu Province and one Tibetan Autonomous Prefecture in Yunnan Province.

Freedom of Religious Belief and Practice in Tibet:

For centuries, Tibetan Buddhism has been a core element of Tibetan culture. The Chinese government has instituted consistent repressive policies against the practice of Tibetan Buddhism with intense regulation and control over religious institutions. This has been demonstrated through "patriotic education", state propaganda and other political campaigns that are fundamentally opposed to the basic doctrine of Tibetan Buddhism, including theatrical attacks on Tibetan religious leaders. Monks are forced to pledge their allegiance to the Chinese government and denounce His Holiness the Dalai Lama which can be dangerous in some of the restive regions in Tibet. Tibetan monasteries and nunneries are required to hang portraits of Chinese communist leaders and the hoisting of Chinese national flag is under the nine measures or Nine Must-Haves campaign[48].

For tightening the control over the religious practice in monasteries, the government-controlled Democratic Management Committee (DMCs) has taken over the administrative role of abbots, and Monasteries. Reportedly, the Chinese government has so far established Monastery Management Committees in 1787 monasteries from 1911 to 2016.[49]

---

[48] Since November 2011, the Chinese authorities begun campaign such as Nine Must Haves and The Six Ones to regulate and restrict the activities
[49] Committees to ensure stability

The worsening religious freedom in Tibet is documented in various global reports, including the annual report of the US Commission on International Religious Freedom, released on 30 April, 2015. The report states that

"The all around repression in China worsened in 2014 including the government aggressiveness in controlling Tibet." "Since 2008, the Chinese government has imposed harsh policies of repression on Tibetan Buddhism across the Tibetan plateau, including harassment, imprisonment, and torture.....self-immolations have continued."

Many, including monks and nuns, have set themselves on fire in the acts of protest.

Thousands of Tibetans, including Buddhist monks, lost their lives in major Tibetan protests against the Chinese occupation of Tibet in 1959, 1987, 1988, 1989 and 2008 to the present. By 1959, discontentment with the Chinese occupation of Tibet had become widespread while culminated in a mass popular uprising in the same year on March 10. This uprising was quickly and brutally suppressed by Chinese troops resulting in more than 90,000 deaths in Lhasa alone. In 2008, over 200 Tibetans were killed, thousands were imprisoned and hundreds simply disappeared.

Thousands of Chinese troops are currently stationed in Tibet and monks and nuns have been subjected to increasingly harsh "patriotic re-education" programmes. Tibetans have been sentenced to lengthy prison terms for advocating for the right to use their language, and the friends and families of Tibetans who have self-immolated have been interrogated and severely punished.

In 2011, Zhu Weiqun, of the CCP United Front, boldly proposed abolishing all reference to nationality on the identity cards that Chinese citizens must carry for inspection. This latest step towards effacing Tibetan identity as a category with legal meaning has not spontaneously appeared. It has a lineage and is best understood in the context of a steady, deliberate, two-sided strategy that has been implemented over the past 20 years. Prior to Weigun's proposal, in 2010, the language of instruction in Tibetan schools was changed from the native language to Chinese. It was met with widespread protest from thousands of students.

But let us accept the proposition that China did warn those Tibetan officials in a recent crackdown. Can that really help the communist regime's cause? Didn't China destroy more than 6,000 monasteries and institutions? Didn't the regime kill at least 1.2 million Tibetans? Didn't they do the same thing in 2008? Didn't the Archbishop Emeritus Desmond Tutu of South Africa end up saying, "China must stop naming, blaming and verbally abusing one whose life has been devoted to non violence, His Holiness the Dalai Lama, a Nobel Peace Laureate"?

From Mao to Hu Jintao, one after the other, the Chinese dictators have taken full control over the lives of their citizens. Today, China is more brutal and inhumane than any other communist regime in the world. The beginning of the 21st century continues to be a time of genocide and violence for the people of Tibet.

China should remember that the immediate cause of the Soviet Union's collapse was ethnic nationalism. Thus China should do all it can to nurture concepts such as ethnic autonomy and self-determination, with special rights and responsibilities guaranteed for legally classified ethnic minorities. Unlike Hong

Kong, Macao or Taiwan, Tibet, as another part of mainland China, is treated in a totally different way.

Freedom of Opinion, Expression and Information:

At present, Tibet is virtually closed and foreign journalists are barred from visiting restive regions. All communication channels, including internet and phone lines are inaccessible or being strictly monitored in regions where protests have occurred. Any independent information or expression other than the Chinese government viewpoints are restricted and considered "subversive". Tibetans who speak to foreign reporters or share information regarding protests through mobile phones or e-mail are charged with "leaking state secrets" and are given lengthy prison sentences.

Tibetan writers, bloggers, singers, teachers, documentary filmmakers and environmentalists are especially targeted since the 2008 Beijing Olympics Games, a year during which over 342 protests took place across the Tibetan plateau.[50] Besides official state media, information received from source outside Tibet are considered offensive and violators are subjected to imprisonment. In a move to clampdown access to information through various foreign radios and television, the Chinese authorities launched a massive crackdown by eradicating satellite dishes and other equipments used by Tibetans.

Freedom to Use and Develop the Tibetan Language:

---

[50] Tibetan's Fierce Objection to Unjust, Brutal and Repressive Rule by China, vol. II, 2012.

Tibetan language plays a crucial role in the preservation of Tibetan culture and distinct Tibetan identity. Schools run privately by Tibetan individuals to teach Tibetans language and culture face severe restrictions.

The Chinese authorities often present their concept of bilingual education as a progressive education policy that confirms their commitment to protect minority cultures and languages. In Tibet bilingual education has generated 'subtractive' bilingualism where Tibetan children are taught only Chinese language, neglecting the native tongue. As reported (China: Minority Exclusion, Marginalization and Rising Tensions) by Human Rights in China, an international Chinese NGO, minority children have limited opportunity to become fluent in their own language.[51] The Tibetan language is increasingly restricted to homes, reducing scope in public sphere-schools, universities and job market, to master one's native language.

Violation of Tibetan Nomads' Rights:

For centuries, Tibetan nomads and herders have lived successfully with their herds using their centuries-old local knowledge and by keeping a mobile lifestyle. However, the current forced 'villagization' policy in the name of development undermines the inherent skills of nomads, restricts their mobility, and raises serious concerns about the long-term socio-economic impact of removing nomads from their traditional form of livelihood without proper and adequate rehabilitation planning.

The grassland rehabilitation policy referred to as the "Restore Grassland", implemented throughout Tibet's nomadic areas, has affected the lives of the nomads. China's measures of resettlement of nomadic herders under different name tags

---

[51] China: Minority Exclusion, Marginalization and Rising Tensions report by Human Rights in China, 2007.

'ecological migrants' or 'comfortable housing projects' are in violation of the International Covenant on Economic, Social and Cultural Rights (ICESCR) and the 1992 Convention on Biodiversity, documents ratified by the People's Republic of China.

Tibetan people have no say in or voice against the hydropower projects that are displacing them from their ancestral lands. The worst-affected Tibetans are mostly illiterate, and live under a climate of fear. They hesitate to raise their voice against government projects. The few brave local leaders who raise their voice, even on environmental grounds, are often convicted of "political motivation." According to Human Rights Watch, the Chinese government asserts that all the relocation and re-housing are entirely voluntary and respect the local Tibetans. However, Tibetans coming from both farming and herding communities interviewed by Human Rights Watch between 2005-2012 say that large number of Tibetans relocated did not do so voluntarily or worse never even consulted.[52] Tibetan villagers in China's Gansu province reportedly staged a sit-down protest against the proposed extension of a Chinese-built highway into nomadic grazing areas. A source revealed that the construction could affect about 700 Tibetan[53] residents and their livelihood. So far the only thing the authorities have done is call the village elders in for questioning and threaten them.

The Chinese government pretentious its radical relocation policies by describing its long-term benefits and claimed that its strategy is succeeding in terms of growing GDP rates in Tibetan Autonomous Region (TAR) higher than national

---

[52] Human Rights Watch, "They Say We should be Grateful," Mass Rehousing and Relocation Programs in Tibetan Areas of China, June 27, 2013.

[53] http://www.rfa.org/english/news/tibet/block-04212015155314.html

average.[54] However, the ground reality is just the opposite with the increase in cost of living, difficulties in integrating into urban economic independence and ineffective employment schemes. In reality, the Tibetan nomads are left worse off than they were before.

Anti-Dalai Lama Campaign:

There was little doubt at that time that Beijing was not interested in dialogue with His Holiness; it only wanted to keep up the pretence to evade international criticism. The adherents of Communist orthodoxy were of the view that His Holiness' return was not necessary to tame the restive Himalayan region. What was needed was a policy of "merciless repression" that harked back to the era of Mao. Chen Kuiyun's appointment as Party Secretary of the Tibet Autonomous Region earlier in 1992 was an indication of that policy. Chen had earned a formidable reputation as a ruthless administrator in Inner Mongolia. He was to remain in Tibet for eight years, during which he successfully tightened China's stranglehold on the neck of Tibetan nationalism.

As the atmosphere of fear engulfed Tibet, Tibetans were becoming increasingly vocal in their opposition to His Holiness' Middle Way approach. Even in His Holiness' own statement, there was a note of despair. In his public statement on 10 March 1994, His Holiness said:

> "I must now recognize that my approach has failed to produce any progress either for substantive negotiations or in contributing to the overall improvement of the situation in Tibet. Moreover, I am conscious of the fact

---

[54] Ibid

that a growing number of Tibetans, both inside as well as outside Tibet, have been disheartened by my conciliatory stand not to demand complete independence for Tibet."

In July that year, Beijing convened the Third Tibet Work Forum, which recommended "relentless blows" to deal with Tibetan nationalist movements, and "life-and-death struggle against the Dalai Clique".

"The struggle between ourselves and the Dalai Clique is neither a matter of religious belief, nor a matter of the question of autonomy, it is a matter of securing the unity of our country and opposing splittism...No one should be careless about it."

To fight the influence of His Holiness, the Forum prescribed a measure that would have been considered adventurous even by Mao himself: reforming the Buddhist religion.

"We must teach and guide Tibetan Buddhism to reform itself. All those religious laws and rituals must be reformed in order to fit in with the needs of development and stability in Tibet. We must reveal the true face of the Dalai hidden behind the religious mask, and prevent by all means and ways the monks and nuns in the monasteries of our region from being affected by the influence of the Dalai clique."

The forum's directive was followed immediately by a dramatic escalation in control and surveillance measures. In 1996 the "Anti-Dalai" campaign was intensified. The photos of His Holiness the Dalai Lama were banned, and people were coerced into criticizing and disavowing loyalty to him. Monks and nuns were sent to jail for resisting the campaign.

<u>**Biased Chinese Media Reporting Creates Ethnic Tension:**</u>

Beijing is using the full might of its propaganda machinery to convince the Chinese people that these protests are anti-Chinese. In a society where the citizens receive news and information from government-controlled media, this is stoking the fire of Chinese nationalism. Beijing has played with this fire before. In 1999 after the Belgrade Chinese embassy bombing, China whipped up anti-American sentiments. China refused to accept President Clinton's initial phone to President Jiang Zemin to apologize. The Chinese Communist Party declared immediately after the bombing through the People's Daily and other media that the bombing had been intentional, not accidental, and supplied buses to transport demonstrators to the U.S. embassy and consulates across China. Anti-Japanese sentiments were whipped up in 2004 and 2005 during the Asian Football Cup matches in China and over the Japanese textbook controversy. The precision with which these protests have flared and just as suddenly died down led many observers to conclude Beijing's hand in organizing them. Both nearly backfired when the protestors shrilly started to criticise the authorities for being weak before the Americans and the Japanese. Fareed Zakaria, editor of Newsweek International, writes

> "In the past they have stoked anti-Japanese and anti-American outbursts, only to panic that things were getting out of control and then reverse course."

This biased reporting on the unrest in Tibet and its negative effect on the Chinese public worries Chinese intellectuals. A group of Chinese scholars, writers and human rights activists wrote a twelve-point letter. In the first point they say,

"At present the one-sided propaganda of the official Chinese media is having the effect of stirring up inter-ethnic animosity and aggravating an already tense situation. This is extremely detrimental to the long-term goal of safeguarding national unity. We call for such propaganda to be stopped."

The second point says,

"We support the Dalai Lama's appeal for peace, and hope that the ethnic conflict can be dealt with according to the principles of goodwill, peace and non-violence. We condemn any violent act against innocent people, strongly urge the Chinese government to stop violent repression and appeal to the Tibetan people likewise to not to engage in violent activities."

In the case of Tibet, the Chinese authorities are stoking ethnic tension in five areas. Agent provocateurs have infiltrated the ranks of Tibetan protestors and indulged in violence to create deep rifts between Tibetans and Chinese. The authorities' relentless demonization of His Holiness the Dalai Lama is hurting Tibetan sentiments. China's brutal crackdown on the Tibetans is sowing the seeds of complete distrust in the authorities. The Chinese government's inflammatory use of the media and biased reporting is creating more misunderstanding amongst the Chinese people. The Chinese government's active encouragement of overseas Chinese students' association to counter pro-Tibet protests with protests of their own is contributing to mutual suspicion.

The responsibility of any government is to provide good governance, including ensuring communal harmony. In fact, President Hu Jintao's stated goal is to create a harmonious society in China. Crackdown and shrill denunciation do not contribute to harmony. China's hardline action to resolve the issue of Tibet has created the biggest rift between Tibetans and Chinese. The crackdown, the enforcement of the "patriotic re-education" and the media focus on the unrest in Tibet are undermining President Hu Jintao's establishment of a harmonious society.

Zhang Boshu of the Chinese Academy of Social Sciences wrote a piece on Tibet called The Way to Resolve the Tibet Issue. Its English translation is posted on www.chinadigitaltimes.net. In his article, Zhang Bozhu writes, 'Hu Yaobang especially stressed:

> "Looking down on Tibetan history, language and art is totally wrong... Loving the minority people is not a matter of empty words. Their social customs and habits must be respected. Respect their language, respect their history, and respect their culture. If you don't do that you are only speaking empty words." Finally, Tibetan cadres should manage Tibet. Within two years, Tibetans should make up two-thirds or more of the cadres in Tibet. "We have been here for thirty years. We have completed our historical mission."
>
> "Today there is 300,000 ethnic Han, including the military, in Tibet."

Monasteries, Weapons and Terrorism:

As the Tibetan protests - popularly known as the March incident - unfolded on the Roof of the World, the Chinese government relied on brute force to silence the Tibetan voices, leading to a large number of peaceful Tibetan demonstrators being arbitrarily arrested, beaten, tortured, killed and disappeared. In order to justify their heinous actions, different functionaries of the Chinese establishment have been spewing various and sundry lies to pass the buck of the unrest in Tibet to His Holiness the Dalai Lama and his exile Administration. China has, employing the full force of its state media and the Public Security Department, ratcheted up its external propaganda efforts to sell its lies to the international community that "large quantities of weapons like guns, knives, spears etc. have been hidden in the monasteries of Tibet, and these bear evidence of the violent nature of the Tibetan people." Having conducted a raid on the Kirti monastery Chinese authorities confiscated 30 guns and 33 swords from that monastery. The piece also alleges that these weapons testify to the Tibetan people's indulgence in violence.

In reality, all these constitute nothing but a mad behavior on the part of the Chinese military to blame the Tibetan people for something they are not responsible for. In a frenzy of madness, they have committed what can be described as an aggravated burglary by making their intrusive entry into the Tibetan monasteries and taking away swords, spears, or other symbolic implements closely associated with the pantheon of wrathful deities - tutelary or protective - belonging to the Tibetan spiritual world. In order to link the Tibetans to violence, the Chinese have also forcibly taken away explosives bought by Tibetan laborers with due permission from the relevant authorities for construction purposes.

Monastic institutions have been not just the centers of learning for the ecclesiastical community; these are also the main repositories of the ancient artefacts and cultural relics of Tibet. Moreover these monasteries are, for the Tibetan people, the ultimate places for seeking spiritual refuge. A monastery has assembly halls, temples, libraries, printing houses, chapels housing protective deities and fierce spirits, etc., all of which have their own unique identities and functions. For example, Protector Shrine is the place where a devotee makes his or her offerings to the protective deities. Here, one will come across numerous wrathful images of Dharmaprotecting and guardian deities. Each of these deities carries symbolic implements such as swords and spears, which is unique to - and identifiable with - that particular deity. These implements are attributed to the concerned deities by historical tradition; it is not something that came into being after the communist Chinese set foot in Tibet.

If the Chinese government is overconfident enough to claim - based on these symbolic implements of the protective deities they have confiscated from the monasteries - that the Tibetan clergy is violence-oriented, then what do they have to say about the Buddhist temples or monasteries in China, where the sculpted images of the Four Worldly Kings, or the Jikas Gods, holding symbolic implements like swords, bow and arrow, long spears, etc., are hung on the doors?

Similarly, in most of the Chinese monasteries, images of Guangong (a historical warrior figure) are erected as local deities or guardians. These images also carry symbolic implements such as long swords and spears. Do these, then, not indicate that Hashangs or the Chinese priests are making preparations for violence?

Looking back into Tibetan history, there were numerous incidents where Tibetan hunters and butchers had pledged to give up their profession of killing or slaughtering animals by willfully offering their weapons such as guns and knives to the monasteries. Likewise, there were many cases where the two feuding communities, families, or even individuals, had decided to end their animosity by offering their weapons to the mediating monasteries. The monasteries, in turn, accept these weapons gladly so that these do not fall in the hands of wrong persons and store or sometimes display them in the chapels housing protective deities and fierce spirits as a way of encouraging other people to tread the same path of non-violence. This tradition among the Tibetan people is indeed laudable. However, the Beijing government presents these very weapons looted from the monastic stores as evidence before the international community to prove that the Tibetan monks are harboring an evil desire to revolt against China. This behavior of the Chinese government is far from being a civilized one but akin to the behaviour of a brigand.

Thus, the Chinese government, while looking down upon, or showing scant respect to, Tibet's unique culture, customs and traditions, etc., goes about doing anything that it feels like doing by conducting raids on the Tibetan monasteries and taking away the treasured possessions, including the statues of deities adorned with expensive jewelry, of these monasteries. Still, Beijing blames the Tibetan clergy for violence, which, in fact, was a peaceful expression of their discontentment. Devoid of truth and reason, this whole drama of having found large quantities of weapons in Tibetan monasteries, as if these monasteries are preparing for a war against the Chinese regime, is nothing but an exaggerated account of the current unrest in Tibet.

Tibetan Youth Congress and Al Qaida:

The state media launched a barrage of propaganda that tried to link some parts of the "Dalai clique" with Al-Qaida and the East Turkestan Independence Movement. A Tibetologist like Liu Hongji wrote a piece in Xinhua, the official news agency, in which he stated, "The TYC has become a terrorist organization as concepts of violence have taken root within it. The group's shadow was evident when the police confiscated a large number of guns and ammunition in some monasteries in China's Tibetan-inhabited regions after the March riot."

We cannot speak on behalf of the Tibetan Youth Congress. The TYC is more than capable of speaking for itself. We are making these comments in so far as China includes the TYC in its broad and all-encompassing term, "the Dalai clique." To call a democratically-elected organisation a "terrorist" with links with Al-Qaida is based on the assumption that those who believe this claim are naives and or is an attempt to harden the Chinese leadership's attitude to the Tibetans. Whatever the real reason for making such absurd claims, the truth is that the TYC is based in India, an open and plural society where free flow of information is cherished. This allows the concerned authorities of India to make an informed judgment of organizations that flout, or does not flout, the laws of the host country. Till now, the Government of India in its considered judgment has not declared the TYC as a terrorist outfit and within the exile Tibetan community the youth body is recognised as a respected organization.

A section of the Chinese leadership's shrill denunciation of the TYC as a terrorist organization stands in sharp contrast to the leadership's dismissive attitude to the same organization in the early 1980's. In those days, the TYC was dismissed as a "fly flapping its wings against the king of the mountains." Now the question is why has a humble fly metamorphosed into a "terrorist" organization in the eyes of the Chinese leaders?

The answer lies with the hardliners in the leadership. They want China, the whole leadership and the Chinese people, to recognize the "Dalai clique" as a "terrorist" organization so that they could deal with it accordingly.

But before the wiser section of the leadership and the Chinese people as a whole are convinced by both the arguments and the evidence produced by the hardliners, they need answers to some questions.

The first question is, if the arms found in the monasteries are truly smuggled by TYC into Tibet under the very noses of the Public Security Ministry, the PLA, the PAP and China's well-placed informers, why weren't transaction prevented in the first place? China has put in place the tightest restrictions on the movement of people, ideas and goods anywhere else in the world. Why did the shipment of such large catchement happen in the first place? Isn't this a major dereliction of duty on the part of China's security forces?

Let us for the sake of argument assume that the TYC was smart enough to ship these arms under the noses of the ever vigilant Chinese security forces into Tibet, why were these let to be allowed into the monasteries without the security forces noticing? The monasteries in Tibet are placed under intrusive survelliance and why was the presence of these weapons in the monasteries not known to the authorities? And why bring out these weapons only when protests took place in Tibet. Isn't it the duty of the security forces to catch "criminals" and expose their "crime" as and when they happen? Why wait this long?

Where were these weapons made? Usually, the brand of the weapons would give clear indication of the source of the weapons. Why has not the spokesperson for the Public Security Ministry informed the international media where the weapons came from?

<u>PLA Soldiers in Monks' Robes:</u>

The Chinese government accuses His Holiness the Dalai Lama of being "a wolf in monk's robes." Ever since the 1959 Tibetan Uprising, the PLA soldiers have been in the habit of doing exactly this: posing as Tibetan monks in order to sow dissension, create distractions and to serve as agents provocateur to incite un-suspecting Tibetan masses into actions that justify quick, military response.

For example, in a book (published in 1992 by the DIIR) about the suffering of the Tibetans in Chinese prisons, a former treasurer of Namgyal Monastery, Venerable Gyaltsen writes that during the 1959 Uprising in Lhasa, Chinese soldiers dressed as Tibetans climbed the Chokpori, next to the Potala Palace and burned incense and strung prayer flags so as to give the impression to the Tibetan public that the Tibetan side had won in the fighting in Lhasa. This was also done to draw out the Tibetan fighters from their hideouts to make it easier for the PLA soldiers to shoot at them.

On 5 March 1988, Tibetans staged a massive protest demonstration on the streets of Lhasa. At the time, the Chinese government ordered a large number of Chinese officials and soldiers to disguise as Tibetan monks and lay Tibetans and deployed them throughout the city. This is based on an account given by Venerable Bhagdro, a former political prisoner.

During the 1989 demonstrations in Lhasa, the Chinese government camp up with the strategy of waging a four-pronged war on Tibetan protestors. As part of this strategy, about 300 Chinese agents and spies were planted within the Tibetan clergy and general public. On the morning of 5 March, they were made to go to the Barkhor and other troubled areas of Lhasa to help the regional and city public security bureaus in deliberately creating disturbances. Their plans included the following:

1 To set aflame the great prayer flag - Gaden Darnyon and Shar Kyareng Darchen - erected at the north-east of the Jokhang Temple.

2. To encourage the local Tibetan residents to destroy and loot the Lhasa Municipality's Grain Store and the Tibet-Gansu Joint Emporia.

This information comes from a book written by Tang Daxian. The book is called The Bayonet Pointed Directly at Lhasa and has been translated into Tibetan and published by the DIIR in 1992

<u>Future of Tibet linked with Sino-Indian Relations:</u>

The future of the Tibet looks inextricably bound up with the state of Sino-Indian relations and in particular with the silent arms race between India and China. It is in the very interest of every concerned party to reveal its legitimate interest in relation to Tibet, and try to convince China of the geographical necessity of a peaceful political solution that would not only minimally satisfy the political aspirations of the Tibetan people but also conciliate the contending security interests of several neighbouring countries including India and the Soviet Union. In this regard, the role of the international community especially that of the superpowers is to exert diplomatic pressure on China.

Tibetan question must not be used for cold war purposes, either old or new variant. It would not be in the long-term interest of any party concerned. For Tibetan people, the African proverb says it well: When the elephants fight, it is only the grass that gets trampled upon.

It is expected of the Chinese leaders or CCP to consider one social fact which appears to be fully borne out by the history of Tibetan civilization. The renowned French Tibetologist R.A. Stein, in his classic study, 'Tibetan Civilization' concludes that the Tibetan case is comparable only with that of Japan. Because the Tibetans did with Buddhism within a span of seven or eight hundred years (8th to 16th century A.D.) is comparable with only what Japan has done since the 19th century with modern science and technology adopted from the West. Both the Japanese and Chinese involve essentially some thinking and its translation into complete products:[55]-monasteries or machines, meditation techniques or medicine, philosophical treatise or technology, thank paintings or photography, merit saving activity or economic investment and so on.

The cultural achievements of Tibetans indicated by their history, whether in war or peace, shows that they are efficient people. They have demonstrated in particular throughout their recorded history that they are efficient enough to rule themselves, though to be sure the Lamaist regimes depended upon either Mongol or Chinese military support. Rehabilitation of Tibetan refugees in South Asia indicates that they are capable of entering the modern world. The Dalai Lam's settlement in Dharmsala is fully manned by bi-lingually educated young Tibetans. The mass of common Tibetan refugees' woollen trade in the whole of India during winter is another clear indication of Tibetan people's sense of enterprise and initiative.

The cultural achievement of Tibet shows that Tibetans are an efficient people, and their history testifies to long periods of self-government and self-rule. During the course of the common dialogue between Dalai Lama and Chinese government, it should be positively considered.

---

[55] Dr. Giriraj Shah, Tibet: The Himalayan Region, Religion, Society and Politics, p. 278.

<u>**Question of Tawang:**</u>

Since the mid-1980s, Chinese negotiators have been demanding that India give them the Tawang tract as part of a border settlement and India has been rejecting the demand. Indian special representatives, who were the serving national security advisors of India (Brajesh Mishra, J.N. Dixit, M.K. Narayanan and Shiv Shankar Menon), had categorically told their Chinese counterparts that to even raise the issue of India ceding Tawang was to indicate that Beijing did not want to really settle the dispute. In other words, the Chinese knew that India will not concede Tawang and yet they kept on raising the idea of a swap involving India conceding Tawang, a major town of the state and a premier centre of Tibetan Buddhism. No Indian government could pass such a deal.

Dai Bingguo, who was Beijing's special representative or top negotiator on the border dispute with his Indian counterparts between 2003 and 2013 insisted that the ball was in the Indian court when he declared that "China and India are now standing in front of the gate towards a final settlement. The gate is a framework solution based on meaningful and mutually accepted adjustments. Now, the Indian side holds the key to the gate." However, China must enter a caveat here: It must be emphasised that Dai is now retired and it is not clear how much, if any, authority his remarks carry.

The issue of Tawang is a complex one. Manoj Joshi, a research fellow, in an article 'Is Tawang Becoming the Focus of Sino-Indian Relations'[56] writes that it is

---

[56] Observer Research Foundation, 09.03.2017.

true, as Dai says that it was culturally Tibetan in that it was the town with one of the great Tibetan monasteries, the place where the fifth Dalai Lama was born. Dai's claim that even the "British colonialists" respected China's jurisdiction over Tawang is ingenuous. The British position, and following it the Indian one, has been that the Tibetans exercised only ecclesiastical authority over the area, not temporal. That has been the Chinese position with regard to the authority of the Dalai Lama in any case.

In 1914, at a time when Tibet was independent, its representative agreed, at a meeting in Shimla, to place it south of the McMahon Line, which was agreed as the border between Tibet and India. A Chinese plenipotentiary who was present in the meetings initialled the agreement, though he did not finally sign it. The Chinese protests thereafter were exclusively about the manner in which McMahon had defined the Tibet-China border, not the India-Tibet boundary.

Communist China also did not raise the issue till 1959. Indeed, in 1962, China occupied Tawang and all of Arunachal Pradesh, but subsequently withdrew behind the border formed by the McMahon Line. This was in contrast to its behaviour in Ladakh, where it did not leave the territory it occupied.

Since the mid-1980s, Indian negotiators have confronted the Chinese claim that the Sino-Indian dispute in the eastern sector was more serious and that India must make concessions, possibly the Tawang tract, in order to resolve the dispute.

Dai's interview is interesting. Last year, he published his memoirs *Strategic Dialogues* and there was no mention of Tawang in it. All he noted was that the "Sino-Indian boundary has never been formally demarcated, but is a traditional customary line formed by the people of the two nations". Refusing to acknowledge the McMahon Line that was created by the Shimla Accord of 1914, he said that the only accepted portion was the Sikkim boundary formed by the 1890 Sino-British convention. The McMahon Line, he insisted was "concocted" by the British and the representatives of the local Tibetan government.

Dai pointed out that the April 2005 agreement on Political Parameters and Agreed Principles for the Settlement of the India-China Border Question was the first political document between the two nations for resolving the border issue.

Article III enjoined on both sides to "make meaningful and mutually acceptable adjustments" with a view of working out "a package settlement to the boundary question." Article IV noted that the two sides should give "due consideration to each other's strategic and reasonable interests." Article V noted that the two sides need to take into account "historical evidence, national sentiments, practical difficulties and reasonable concerns and sensitivities." Article VII said that both sides "shall safeguard due interests of their settled populations in the border areas."

A simple reading of its clauses would suggest that the guidelines would eventually lead to a more or less "as is where is" position. The only viable package was allegedly suggested by Zhou Enlai in 1960 and Deng Xiaoping in 1980 – that in exchange for India surrendering its claim of Aksai Chin, China would concede its claim on Arunachal Pradesh.

Article IV would suggest that India would do it on the basis of accepting Aksai Chin as a strategic interest for China, while the latter would agree to do the same in the case of Arunachal on the basis of Article VII.

Up to the advent of the internet, the regime had been able to successfully curtail this freedom in nearly all its physical manifestations. Beijing has a tightly controlled traditional media, while forcing all published information to be from official sources and to be vetted through the state control.

Ironically, the regime founded on the free speech-backbone of Marx's words stipulates a minimum personal income of $35,000 to be able to publish print media, an income level which could easily be considered bourgeois by Chinese standards. China also has strong restrictions against assembly and worship, demonstrated over the last few days with a crackdown on Tibetan protesters.

Many assumed the government's ability to crack down on dissent would be destroyed by the increased prominence of a dynamic and nearly infinite internet space. However, China has adapted its censorship policies to the internet, and by many standards managed to stay ahead of the curve in restricting free speech in the digital realm.

Internet use in China is blossoming. As of recent survey, the so called China Internet Network Information Centre, considered the premier source for measuring Chinese internet use, pegged the number of Chinese users at 210 Million. This number will only grow in the foreseeable future, with the booming mobile market, more and more a popular portal to the internet, estimated to hit more than 600 Million by 2014. This realm has been modified from its original version. It has been formatted to fit The Party's view of the world.

China has responded with a vast centralized censorship program. One study by a group at Harvard in 2002, "found blocking of almost every kind of content. If it exists, China blocks sites at least some of it." The blocking has traditionally been centred on political and opinion based sites. Some of the most likely to be blocked are related to independence movements in Tibet, Taiwan and Hong Kong, protest groups like the Falun-Gong, political parties opposed to the regime, and sites on democracy and human rights.

For the majority of Chinese web-users, these controversial topic-specific sites are not part of their daily internet routine, which focuses merely on sports, entertainment and gaming sites. These users may have only the vaguest notion of the filtering being conducted by the state, including internet cafes being required to record and store information about all users and their internet use. Recently, however, the Great Firewall of China has evoked increased backlash as it has begun to block more popular social media sites such as Facebook, Twitter, Flickr and selected MySpace pages.

China's filtering and censorship program is regarded as the most sophisticated in the world. It includes some 30,000 censors as well as technology, often provided by foreign companies like Yahoo who are required to censor their results or be censored themselves. The filtering effort is in conjunction with a strict criminal prosecution system working with laws that forbid the publication of anything:

i. Denying the guiding status of Marxism, Mao Zedong Thought, or Deng Xiaoping Theory;

ii. Violating the Party line, guiding principles, or policies;

iii. Anything else that violates Party propaganda discipline or violates national publishing administration regulations.

Making unrefuseable conditions, the regime also forces companies to display propaganda content. All ISPs are legally required to abide by these rules.
When we look on a wider perspective, North Korea has a reputation as one of the most secret nations in the world and for international journalists; it's one of the

hardest places from which to report. But surprisingly there's a place that allows even fewer foreign reporters than North Korea does: China-controlled Tibet. That's according to Tibet scholar Carole McGranahan, who is a professor of the University of Colorado at Boulder and who made the point during a recent lecture at Yale University, video of which is embedded below. McGranahan also discussed the rising trend of Tibetan self-immolations - a form of political protest against Chinese rule - and the challenge of understanding Tibet's turmoil.

Beijing's near-total isolation of Tibet makes it awfully difficult for the outside world to see or understand what is happening there. Presumably, that's part of the point; Chinese rule in Tibet can be shockingly severe, as can the ongoing efforts to assimilate Tibetan people and culture into the rest of China.

The so called moderating China has no interest in whether conforming to the platitudes of free speech, human rights, press and dissent nor those espoused by Marx, Mao and its own constitution. While dissent may seem compatible within the framework of theoretical communism, it appears to be at odds with the communism practiced in China. In revoking its founder's statements, the government's position may seem to oppose the spirit of communism; yet, the choices make perfect sense when considered in the framework of decision-making without eethical considerations, like democracies aspire to do, rather on the basis of what is best for the communist regime.

However, the Paris based global media-watch-dog 'Reporters without Borders' said "There can be no justification for remaining silent in the face of these flagrant violations of freedom of information, not even the 'respect for sovereignty' that the Chinese government repeatedly cites in response to criticism of its repressive and discriminatory policies towards Tibetans."

The media watch-dog in its annual "Enemies of the Internet" index, which has highlighted China as one of the worst violators of press freedom and one of the Internet's biggest enemies, still holds among the lowest rankings in recent years.

While moving away from the one-man-dictatorship of Mao's days, President Xi Jinping is unlikely to make the same mistakes made by those formers who have wanted to maintain China's crony capitalism using the Maoist iron fist. What the Chinese people have been hoping for is a change in the philosophy of ruling China with an autocratic, totalitarian regime. But will Xi continue to follow the same six decade old-system in future? It's a big question for everyone.

CHAPTER IV

INDIA'S APPROACH TO THE TIBETAN QUESTION

Despite a booming bilateral trade, the strategic discord and rivalry between China and India are sharpening. Tibet is a key factor in Sino-Indian relations. It is only after the 1950 Chinese occupation of Tibet that India and China came to share the disputed common border. Even during the 1962 conflict, Chinese leaders, including Mao, acknowledged that the conflict was not about the boundary or territory but Tibet.

The revolt in Tibet leading to the flight of the Dalai Lama to India in 1959 came as a rude shock to the Indian leadership. After the 1962 conflict, the issue of Tibet was kept on the back burner. The revival of negotiations in 1981 brought the issue back into focus. The Chinese consistently tried to obtain reassurances from India that the Indian position on Tibet be reverted to before, and that India would stop "meddling" in Tibetan affairs and would control the activities of the Dalai Lama in India.

Recently, China's military build-up and infrastructural development in Tibet and reported plans to divert rivers flowing into India and constructing dams on them (like Brahmaputra etc.), have been concerning India. On the other hand, China is insecure that the presence of the Dalai Lama and Tibetan refugee population in India will create issues for China in Tibet. The presence of the Dalai Lama and Tibetan refugees in India keeps the "Tibetan Question" alive.

India has an open democratic system and has been providing shelter to persecuted people for ages. Taking this into consideration, India finds it difficult to meet China's expectation on Tibet without a favour or advantage granted in return. Lately, China's aggressive territorial claims on India, the deepening of the China-Pakistan alliance and a shift in China's position on Kashmir have led to India hardening its position on Tibet. Thus in the recent times very evidently Indian foreign and defence policies from being Pak-centric to becoming Sino-centric.

Question of Tibet's future seems to still in the air, not quite dead or as lively as in 1960. At first the Beijing-Dalai Lama meeting in 1986 gave birth to some prospects for a peaceful political settlement but that also proved unsuccessful. The Chinese are in a position dictate terms to the Dalai Lama. They have occupied the country and are militarily in control of their subjects. China since the Sino-American detente has emerged as a great Asian power to be feared. All these changes in favour of China have tended to put the Tibetan question, purely in rational terms, in a hopeless position.

Tibet occupies the central position in Sino-India relations, so much so that, it will not be an exaggeration to say that Sino-Indian relations have been taken hostage by the Tibet's embarrassing situation. Without resolving the Tibetan issue, Sino-Indian ties cannot be stabilised. Therefore, resolution of Tibet issue to the satisfaction of Tibetan people, China and India, is a pre-condition for better Sino-Indian relations.

This suggests that international relations are too complex to be viewed in simple bilateral ties; there are hosts of intervening factors that modify or reshape policies, which in turn are mediated by domestic politics and transnational political structures. India is now seeking satisfaction on what it considers to be a core issue to its sovereignty and territorial integrity. Sino-India relations are unlikely to be on an even keel until this tangled knot is unravelled.

Historically Tibet has served as a buffer zone between India and China. In 1959, China occupied Tibet and since then the border has became a contentious issue between India and China. The Indian Prime Minister Jawaharlal Nehru made substantial efforts to create peace with China and they reached an agreement, which is known as the Panchsheela agreement. This was Nehru's strategy to build a partnership with China to consolidate the non-alignment movement in the world. This Sino-India partnership did not last very long. In 1962, China launched a war against India and India lost 3270 Indian soldiers. This was an unprecedented defeat for India and a huge victory for China. Thus both countries suspended their diplomatic relations. Later in 1979 the countries restored their diplomatic relations and they exchanged a head of the states visit. But in 1998, when India tested its first nuclear weapon, China strongly condemned. Again the diplomatic relations between the two countries were suspended but they resumed again in 2005. In 2005 Chinese Premier Wen Jiabao visited India and established trade relations and strategic dialogue regarding the border dispute. The trade between the two has progressed but border dialogue has not made any notable progress. There has been indirect competition between the two in the North of India and in South East Asia. China has been rapidly advancing its military bases towards the Northern border of India and making its presence in the seaports in South East Asia. India and China are hugely different in terms of political ideology and culture. Due to these issues, confrontation between the two in the future is inevitable.

Sino-Indian Relations: History, Problems and Prospects:

The history of the Sino-Indian relations began in 1949 when India became the first non-communist state who recognised the People's Republic of China (PRC) as the legitimate government of China. Jawaharlal Nehru was the Indian Prime Minister and was the founding architect of Indian foreign policy, which vigorously opposed global military alignment. India supported the new independent states of Asia to pursue a policy of non-alignment. This was a core Indian foreign policy to approach any other states including China. India viewed China as an essential partner for India to strengthen the non-alignment movement in the world. On the eve of India's independence, Nehru expressed an "Asian Monroe Doctrine," which described a complete removal of the Western militaries from Asia, for which cooperation with China was vital. Therefore, Nehru actively engaged with China in the 1950s and as a result India signed an agreement with China, which was known as 'Panchsheela' or 'five principles', of peaceful coexistence between two nations. In that agreement, India supported the one China policy, which stated that Tibet was a part of the PRC. From 1949 to 1959, these two nations maintained a decade long good relationship. This period was described as "Hindi Chini Bhai Bhai" which meant that Indians and Chinese were brothers. However, this period of peace came to an end when China ruthlessly cracked down on Tibetan protestors in Lhasa on the 10th March 1959, forcing the Dalai Lama and the Tibetan peoples to flee to India. India granted refugee status for the Dalai Lama and Tibetan people in India. Thus the relationship between India and China worsened and it led to the 1962 War between India and China.

The 1962 war between India and China deeply impacted the contemporary Sino-Indian relations. Under Prime Minister Jawaharlal Nehru's leadership, India played a leadership role among Asian nations. The Bandung Conference was held in Indonesia in 1955. Jawaharlal Nehru dominated the session by proposing five principles of foreign policy, which were non-alignment, anti-colonialism, anti-racism, peaceful coexistence and respects others' territorial integrity. There were twenty-nine state representatives who participated in the conference and all the members unanimously supported Nehru's proposal. India gained a substantial legitimacy over international affairs. At the same time the Asian nations expected to see leadership from India and India also claimed itself as a dominant power in Asia. However, in the 1962 Sino-India war, China defeated India militarily and psychologically. The war went for thirty-two days and left thousands of Indian soldiers dead, and it proved that India was militarily in a weak position. Therefore, many Asian nations turned away from India because they saw India was unable to provide security for them. India lost its credibility as a great international power indeed, and had to live with great humiliation. This was the worst period in the history of the Sino-Indian relations.

It has been widely noted by political scientists that the coexistence of India and China in the international state system is highly unusual in that they both aspire to superpower status and share a border. Fifty years ago, this border was both casus belli and battleground between the two countries. Today, it remains the source of multiple disputes. Yet the Sino-Indian border, like the wider relationship between the two countries, can just as easily be characterized as being relatively peaceful. This has been the view of many in the diplomatic community on both sides.

Speaking in the 1990s, AK Damodaran, an Indian Foreign Service officer and China expert, argued that "the fact that this troubled border between the two countries had only three incidents in thirty years suggests that this is one of the quieter borders in the world." Two decades later, the border remains remarkably quiet, given that the underlying disputes remain unresolved.

While the cultural ties between China and India go back to over two millennia, independent India and the People's Republic of China were born within three years of each other in the late 1940s. India was one of the earliest nations to recognize the PRC, rather than the Taiwan-based Republic of China, as a sovereign state. In the midst of the Korean War, Indian diplomats at the United Nations proposed UN membership for the PRC as a necessary part of any ceasefire. While the popular Hindi slogan of "Hindi-Chini Bhai Bhai" (Indo-Chinese friendship) contained an element of exaggeration, relations during the early and mid-1950s were broadly congenial. Yet while Prime Minister Jawaharlal Nehru and Zhou Enlai, his Chinese counterpart, were publicly committed to this project, as symbolized by the 1954 Panchsheela Agreement, which effectively symbolized Indian acceptance of Chinese control of Tibet, it was soon undermined by three distinct disputes.

India's border with China, its longest with any neighbour, was complicated both by China's acquisition of Tibet and by the fact that the agreements governing the border line had been drawn up by officials of the British Empire. The border between India and Tibet, the McMahon line, had never formally been recognized by China, which now coveted Aksai Chin, a portion of eastern Ladakh in the Indian state of Jammu and Kashmir, as a means to link Tibet and Xinjiang by road. Additionally,

China claimed the region controlled by India south of the eastern end of the McMahon Line, an area then administered as the North-East Frontier Agency (NEFA) and now as the state of Arunachal Pradesh, but known to the Chinese as South Tibet. This area had historically been claimed by Lhasa, but was ceded by Tibet; in the 1913-14 Shimla Agreement saw the drawing of the McMahon Line.

This soon proved impossible. In 1958, Indian officials became aware of significant Chinese encroachment across the Johnson Line (claimed by India as the international border) in the nearly uninhabited Aksai Chin. The Chinese had commenced building a highway from Tibet to Xinjiang through Aksai Chin, in what was then Indian Territory. A few months later, Chinese maps began to display Aksai Chin as part of China. Indian outrage at this provocation was counterbalanced by Chinese anger at India's decision to grant asylum to the fourteenth Dalai Lama, who fled Tibet in 1959 after a failed anti-Chinese uprising, falsely suspected by the PRC to be a CIA-orchestrated operation. Both sides felt betrayed, and a heated exchange of letters between Nehru and Zhou over the next three years was the inevitable precursor to armed conflict.

The Sino-Indian War of 1962 was, in military terms, a humiliating defeat for the Indians. For several years, KS Thimmaya, India's Chief of Army Staff, and several others in Delhi had warned of a lack of preparedness in the face of Chinese aggression. India's Defence Minister, the fiercely anti-Western VK Krishna Menon, chose to ignore these warnings, with dire consequences; India was routed on both the western (Aksai Chin) and eastern (NEFA) fronts. In the face of opposition from both superpowers, the Chinese swiftly withdrew, but only after securing all of Aksai Chin. The Chinese withdrawal, however, left NEFA in Indian hands.

The 1962 war transformed Indian foreign and security policy. Two years later China tested a nuclear device, and India was compelled to accelerate investment in its own nuclear program. India's nuclear test of 1974 was just as much a response to the Chinese threat as to the Pakistani one. China was the only nuclear power in Asia, and much of the groundwork for India's test was initiated in the immediate aftermath of the 1962 war. The near-simultaneous events of the war and the Sino-Soviet split ensured, by the early 1970s, that the Sino-Indian rivalry was now a part of the global Cold War. India signed a Friendship Treaty with the Soviet Union in 1971, while China normalized relations with the United States and developed close ties with Pakistan, a key US ally and India's chief opponent. Yet the aid provided by China to Pakistan during its wars with India in 1965 and 1971 was far too small to alter military outcomes in either case, particularly in India's decisive victory of 1971. Nonetheless, India's growing closeness to the Soviet Union can justifiably be interpreted as, in part, a response to Sino-Pakistani cooperation. The Sino-Soviet split also had an impact on Indian domestic politics: it was the proximate cause of the split in the Communist Party of India (CPI), which had heretofore assumed the responsibility of the opposition to the ruling Indian National Congress.

The election of the Janata Party in 1977, India's first non-Congress government and the contemporary rise of Deng Xiaoping in China saw a marked, although gradual, improvement in relations. Diplomatic ties had been restored a year later in 1976 when the Chinese eventually responded to Indian overtures first made in 1969, but the new governments in both countries departed from the previous policy of placing Sino-Indian relations in the contexts of Sino-Soviet and Indo-Pakistani conflicts. The Janata government was more genuinely non-aligned than pro-Soviet, and Deng Xiaoping, for his part, even suggested the possibility of a Chinese acknowledgment of Indian sovereignty over NEFA in exchange for India's relinquishing of its claim to Aksai Chin. While such measures have never been adopted, a similar principle motivated the 1993 and 1996 agreements on a Line of Actual Control. In 1996, Jiang Zemin made a state visit to India; several such visits have followed since.

The Sino-Indian diplomatic relationship was restored between the two countries in 1976. The ambassadors were restored in both countries' capitals and the ambassadors attempted to make improvements to the relationship by establishing further diplomatic exchange. In 1979, Indian foreign minister Mr Atal Behari Vajpayee visited China and he signed an agreement, which stated that both countries promised to keep peace in the region. In 1988, Indian Prime Minister Rajiv Gandhi visited China. This was the highest Indian politician to visit China since the 1962 war. This was a turning point and both countries hoped it would improve their relationship beyond the war. Indeed, both countries began to look forward to developing their relations. In 1991, the Chinese Premier Li Peng visited India and then in 1993, the Indian Prime Minister Narasimha Rao went to China. In 1993, the Chinese President Jiang Zemin visited India, marking the first time a Chinese head of state had visited India. During Jiang's visit, they agreed to build a constructive and cooperative relationship based on the five principles of peaceful co-existence. Above all, the diplomatic exchanges demonstrate that both countries fully restored a diplomatic relationship after the 1962 war. However, there was no progress with regard to border and security issues.

India carried out its first nuclear test in 1998 and this overturned its diplomatic relationship with China. China vigorously condemned India's nuclear test and China took the lead in drafting the UN's Security Council Resolution 1172, which strongly condemned the tests. India understood the consequences of testing nuclear weapons without the United Nations' permission but the Indian politicians considered it absolutely necessary to demonstrate India's security capabilities. China and Pakistan were a potetial security threat to India and India viewed the security threat from these countries as inevitable. However, it resulted in China immediately suspending its diplomatic relations with India, viewing India's nuclear test as a security threat. For two years there were no diplomatic engagements between the two countries. This was the second period in which the complex Sino-India relationship was damaged badly.

<u>Issue of Tibet</u>:

Over many years His Holiness, the Dalai Lama did his best to engage the Chinese leadership in an honest dialogue. Unfortunately, a lack of political will and vision on the part of the Chinese leadership resulted in their failure to reciprocate the numerous initiatives of His Holiness. Finally, in August 1993 the Tibetan leadership's formal contact with the Chinese government came to an end.

Since then to September 2002, the two sides did not have any formal and direct contact. It was only on 9 September 2002 that Beijing hosted a four-member Tibetan delegation, headed by Special Envoy Lodi G. Gyari. During the visit, the delegates met a number of Chinese and Tibetan leaders both in China and Tibet. As outlined in the press statement issued by the delegation on their return from Beijing, the purpose of the visit was two-fold: One, to re-establish direct contacts with the leadership in Beijing and to create a conducive atmosphere for direct face-to-face meetings on a regular basis; Two, to explain His Holiness the Dalai Lama's Middle Way Approach towards resolving the issue of Tibet.

In order to sustain the new contact, the same delegation visited China and Tibetan areas for the second time from 25 May to 8 June 2003. The visit followed the changes in leadership of the Chinese Communist Party as well as of the Chinese Government and had given the delegation the opportunity to engage extensively with the new Chinese leaders and officials responsible for Tibet and relationship with the leaders of the Tibetan people in exile. In Beijing the delegation met with Ms. Liu Yandong, head of the United Front Work Department of the Communist Party of China, Mr. Zhu Weiqun, deputy head, Mr. Chang Rongjung, the Deputy Secretary-General, and other senior officials.

The Tibetan delegation had the third round of meetings with their Chinese counterpart in Beijing in September 2004. At this meeting, both sides acknowledged the need for more substantive discussions in order to narrow down the gaps and reach a common ground. This was followed by the fourth round of meetings that took place on 30 June and 1 July 2005 at the Embassy of the People's Republic of China in Berne, Switzerland. Special Envoy Lodi G. Gyari and Envoy Kelsang Gyaltsen, accompanied by three senior assistants, Sonam N. Dagpo, Ngapa Tsegyam, and Bhuchung K. Tsering, met with Vice Minister Zhu Weiqun and his six-member delegation. Vice Minister Zhu declared that their direct contact with the Tibetan delegation had now become stable and an "established practice." He also conveyed to the Tibetan delegation that the Central leadership of the Chinese Communist Party attached great importance to the contact with His Holiness the Dalai Lama. The Tibetan side put forward some concrete proposals that will help build trust and confidence and move the ongoing process to a new level of engagement aimed at bringing about substantive negotiations to achieve a mutually acceptable solution to the Tibetan issue.

Meanwhile, in order to resolve the issue of Tibet on the basis of His Holiness the Dalai Lama's Middle-Way Approach, the Central Tibetan Administration (CTA) has made every effort within its power to create a conductive atmosphere for negotiations and taken a series of confidence-building measures. The CTA is committed to take these steps till the issue of Tibet is resolved through a negotiated settlement in the best interest of both the Tibetan and Chinese peoples

Sino-Indian diplomatic relations resumed in 2000 when the Chinese foreign minister visited India and met with the Indian foreign minister to start a security dialogue. In 2005, the Chinese Premier Wen Jiabao visited India, which was a historic visit because the Premier upgraded the bilateral ties to a strategic level. Premier Wen's visit produced three points. Firstly, India and China agreed on a strategic and cooperative partnership for peace and prosperity in both countries. Secondly, they agreed to establish political guiding principles for the settlement of the disputed boundary issue. Thirdly, they created a five year plan for all-round cooperation and trade between the two countries. Premier Wen's visit was extraordinarily successful. In the following year Chinese President Hu Jintao visited India, which consolidated the bilateral ties between the two countries. Hu stated that "building trust through trade" was necessary and also declared that the two countries were "not rivals or competitors but partners for mutual benefit." During this visit,

President Hu and Indian Prime Minister Manmohan Singh agreed to expand their trade target to $20 billion by 2008._China became India's largest trading partner in 2008 and it overtook the United States. The trade between the two countries is increasing and diplomatic visits between the two have become quite regular, including heads of the state. However, the core issues between Sino India of the border and security have so far not made any progress.

In recent years, the Chinese military have asserted claims over Indian controlled territories. Ladakh and Arunachal Pradesh have frequently had Chinese military incursions. Thus, the Indians view the Chinese emerging power not as a peaceful one, but one that poses a serious security threat to India. India sees the China and Pakistan alignment as a form of security threat to her. India also has ongoing extensive border disputes with Pakistan. Thus China and Pakistan's nuclear cooperation is a clear indication to India that China is trying to indirectly undermine India's stability. China has increased its influence over India's neighbours such as Nepal, Bhutan, Sri Lanka and Myanmar. Historically these countries were strongly influenced by India. Nepal, Bhutan and Sri Lanka have historically and culturally been entangled with India. However, in recent years, China has been aggressively engaging with these countries by providing unconditional and vast aid. China is Myanmar's largest trading partner and China has supported the military dictatorship in Myanmar for decades. This shows that China is strategically and geographically circling around India from land borders to the sea. China is preparing itself for India to be its major rival and competitor in Asia in the twenty first century.

The competition between India and China is inevitable in the 21th century in Asia. Historically both countries had been dominant empires in Asia throughout such periods as the Chinese Ming Empire and the Indian Mughal Empire. Today, China and India both want to restore their position in the world like their previous empires. China is already claiming it is a great world power and it is on its way to world super power status. China is the world's second largest economy with a 1.3 billion population. According to the Fugel estimate, China will overtake the United States by the year 2040 and it will become the world's largest economy. China gained nuclear status in 1964 when it first tested a nuclear weapon. China is also rapidly modernising its military force by pumping a vast part of the budget into its military program. China developed its first aircraft carrier in 2013 and built aircrafts. The Chinese built the J-15, which is the newest model that China launched in 2010. Compared to China, India is far behind in terms of economic progress and modernising its military force. However, India tested its first nuclear weapon in 1998 and it is part of the world nuclear club. India has also developed a robust military personal with adequate war equipment. India's economic growth is not as fast as the Chinese economy but it is one of fastest developing economies in the world. Both China and India claim to be the giant powers in Asia. This will be the challenge for the twenty first century in Asia to keep these two countries peacefully co-existing.

India and China are such different countries politically and culturally. India exercises freedom of expression and rights of civil liberty. India runs the freest media and this plays a significant role in its politics. On the other hand, China is different from India in terms of its political system and its culture. The communist party decides who governs the country and civilians have no voice in the Chinese political system. In China there is also no freedom of expression. States own the media and independent media is not allowed and thus the Chinese people are heavily influenced by the government's control. The Chinese government claims that this authoritarianism is suitable for China because Chinese culture is rooted in Confucianism. Confucius views that the state owns absolute authority over its people. These fundamental differences between India and China will pose certain challenges in Asia. This creates unforgettable resentment in public and vast numbers of Indian politicians views China as India's ultimate security threat in the 21st century. China is rapidly increasing its influence around India's neighbours such as Pakistan, Nepal, Bhutan Myanmar and Sri Lanka. This is a form of an indirect confrontation between India and China.

The Dalai Lama advised that Government of India must study the issue of Tibet thoroughly and from a wider perspective, failing which India will face a new and grave danger. Because, if the present situation continues, for India, the problems are only going to multiply. If the Government of India takes a stronger stand on the issue of Tibet she will be able to eliminate the danger of the present Chinese threat from Tibet. This will also help to diminish the dangers being posed by India's neighbours on the west and the east, two nations who cannot be a threat without the support of China.

A strong stand on Tibet will obviously strain Indo-Chinese relations temporarily. And for a moment it may also appear odd that India should take a hard position against China when the latter is becoming more moderate and practically everyone else is rushing to establish relations with her. A stand must now be taken or it may be too late. Economically, India need not suffer much. There is substantial trade between India and China. Even if the overall relations become strained trade relations could continue. Militarily, it is quite certain there will be no danger of war being waged on India by China. In the 1962 Indo-Chinese war the Chinese, in spite of their initial successes, unilaterally ceased fire and withdrew. They were compelled to do these because apart from having to transport men and material over hundreds of miles of hostile territory they were fully aware that ultimately they had no hopes of being victorious over India. The situation today remains unchanged, if it has not become more difficult for the Chinese.

The condemnation of the violation of the fundamental rights of a people anywhere is not considered as interference in the internal affairs of another country. Even if the Government of India presently accepts Tibet to be a nominal part of the People's Republic of China, India has a natural and moral responsibility for the Tibetan people because of India's unique relationship with Tibet. China has physically dominated the Tibetans but the Tibetans look towards India with great hope and faith. Even purely in practical terms the issue of Tibet is of extreme importance to India. However, if the Tibetans gradually leave their spiritual nature and become more Communist, China's grip on Tibet will be further strengthened. In view of these, it is only pragmatic for India to take full advantage of the situation, especially since the border issue between India and China still remain unresolved.

It is, therefore, in the interest of India, as well as in the interest of world peace, to support the rights of the Tibetan people. India has to review its past policies and reconsider the issue of Tibet. For which some measures to followed are:

1. The minimum that we must strive for is genuine autonomy for the entire area of Tibet. It should be autonomy according to international law and not according to the Chinese version.

2. Maintain Tibet as a 'zone of peace' or 'zone of ahimsa' and ensure the absence of any military presence there.

3. All Chinese troops must be withdrawn from Tibet or else a limit must be set on the number of troops to be stationed.

4. Indian troops will have to continue patrolling the borders.

5. The right to self-determination of a people is widely accepted by an enlightened world and Tibetans have this right too.

Government of India has already voted in favour of the U.N. General Assembly's resolution on Tibet in 1965. Government of India supported the Tibetan people's right to self-determination. Some people have the view that support for Tibetan people's right to self-determination will put the Government of India in a difficult position in dealing with the Kashmir issue. But according to international law, there is vast difference between these two issues.

Tibetans are striving for the independence of Tibet- historically, culturally, geographically, racially and in many other ways Tibet and China are different. Because of these differences, Tibet remained independent in the past and even today 95% of the Tibetan people aspire for complete independence. The struggle for Tibetan independence is a just cause and the status of Tibet is of real importance to her neighbours.

The aim of Tibet's independence cannot be ignored or neglected, because according to international law it is still an independent nation under illegal Chinese occupation and the Tibetan Government-in-exile is the rightful and legitimate Government of the Tibetan people and nation. There are references to the issue of Tibet which must be made from time to time in the U.N. Assembly as well as in the

Commission of Human Rights. Issue related to culture and religion should be raised in the UNESCO. An appropriate opportunity must be seized to have resolution on Tibet adopted in the Non-Aligned movement.

Throughout the world many Tibetan religious centres have been established. It is possible to create a new interest in the issue of Tibet through these centres. Number of offices in different counties, New York, Tokyo, London, Winterthur and many more, are working for the Tibetan issue.

After the Chinese policy of liberalisation, there are still many Tibetans who continue to come to India. Along the Indian border from Ladakh to Arunachal Pradesh, Tibetan refugees have been turned back and forced to return to Tibet. Government of India does not allow their entry. Quite a number are able to come through Nepal, particularly the young who are keen to acquire education. All this clearly shows that the situation in Tibet is neither normal nor satisfactory for the Tibetan people.

The Third Tibet Work Forum and the Seeds of the Tibetan Crisis:

From July 20 to 23, 1994, Beijing staged the Third Forum on work in Tibet, which recommended the total destruction of an entire civilization flourishing on the Tibetan plateau for thousands of years. The Third Forum on Tibet was convened by the top Chinese leadership and was presided over by the then President Jiang Zemin. The authorities have now enshrined this Work Forum as the most "important strategic policy to rejuvenate Tibet" and have hailed its directives as the new manifesto for party work on the plateau.

The significance of the Third Work Forum lies in the fact that it overturned the more liberal policies laid out for Tibet's "development" by the First and Second Work Forums held in 1980 and 1984. The first two work forums were initiated by the late Hu Yaobang, then Secretary General of the Chinese Communist Party. This liberal leader is credited with masterminding a series of measures to improve the social, economic and political conditions in Tibet. The brief spell of liberalization markedly improved the living conditions of the majority of Tibetans and contributed to a more relaxed intellectual and social climate.

All these were reversed at the Third Work Forum. The Third Work Forum policy recommendations contained four key elements. China stepped up the scale of repression in Tibet. External propaganda work was escalated. The pace of economic development in Tibet and its corollary of encouraging more Chinese settlers and businessmen to take advantage of the economic boom on "the roof of the world" were also increased.

The main target of the current policy of repression is Tibetan Buddhism. Chinese leaders are increasingly alarmed by the proliferation of monasteries and temples which in the period of liberalization spawned throughout Tibet: they are seen as the bastions of Tibetan nationalism. The authorities have set up "Democratic Management Committees" to control monasteries and nunneries and established "Work Inspection Teams" to supervise the "education" of monks and nuns.

What appeals the Tibetan people is China's all-out war on Tibetan culture. The leadership revived the old aphorisms once served up to the Tibetan people to justify their policies to destroy Tibetan Buddhism during the Cultural Revolution. Bewildered Tibetans were then told that just as there cannot be two suns in the sky, so there could not be both Buddhism and socialism in Tibet. Inevitably Buddhism had to give way to socialism. Today Buddhism is once again being blatantly sublimated to Chinese state power.

A major thrust is underway to break the bond of loyalty between the clergy in Tibet and His Holiness the Dalai Lama in India. Campaigns like "Strike Hard" and "Patriotic Re-education", unleashed in 1996, are aimed at crippling the rise of Tibetan Buddhism which the authorities suspect is weaning the loyalty of the Tibetan people away from the communist party and towards His Holiness the Dalai Lama.

One salient feature of the "Strike Hard" campaign is how differently it is interpreted in China and Tibet. China's "Strike Hard" campaigns was started to weed out crime. Tibet's version was used as a political tool to eliminate those whom the authorities label "splittists". In Tibet, rather than combating crime, the authorities turn a blind eye to this social disease in the hope that it will erode the traditional morality of Tibetans and undermine Tibetan Buddhism.

In fact, at a secret meeting held in December 1999 in Chengdu, capital of Sichuan province, Chen Kuiyuan, the hardline Party Secretary of "TAR" recommended to the Central Chinese Government that an all-out effort must be made to eradicate Tibetan Buddhism and culture from the face of the earth so that no memory of them will be left in the minds of coming generations of Tibetans- except as museum pieces.

Chen Kuiyuan stated that the main cause of instability is the existence of the Dalai Lama and his Government-in-Exile in Dharamsala and this must be "uprooted". He recommended that Tibet, Tibetan people and Tibetan Buddhism - in other words the very name of Tibet - must be destroyed and the "Tibet Autonomous Region" be merged with provinces like Sichuan.

This total assault on Tibetan culture is heightened by comments made by the current party secretary in Tibet. Zhang Qingli said, "The communist party is like parents to the Tibetan people and are always considerate about what the children need. The party is the real Buddha for the Tibetans." On His Holiness the Dalai Lama Zhang Qingli said, "The Dalai is a devil with a human face but with a heart of a beast. Those who do not love their country are not qualified to be human beings." On the Tibetan struggle for greater freedoms, Zhang Qingli said, "We are currently in an intensely bloody and fiery struggle with the Dalai clique, a life-and-death struggle with the enemy."

There are different views within the leadership regarding how to handle the issue of Tibet. Mark Maginer, reporting for the Los Angeles Times in a report says, "And Beijing is making more use of good-cop, bad-cop tactics. On the issue of Tibet, for instance, some arms of the government decried the Dalai Lama, the exiled Tibetan spiritual leader, even as other parts called for negotiations."

That there are two schools of thought in the Chinese central government on how to handle the issue of Tibet is admitted by the Chinese state media. For example, China's official news agency, Xinhua, in its commentary by Yi Yan, republished on its website, www.chinaview.cn of 1 July 2008 admits this. The commentary is entitled "The Choice for Dalai Lama". It says,

> "If the Dalai Lama wrongly gauges the support the West gives him, and takes for granted the good intentions of the central government, or tries to seek a prey that is beyond reason, or even encourage and instigate his radical

followers to engage in violence, once again, Beijing will surely be enraged. Under this circumstance, it will force the central government to give up on him, once and all. There exists such advocacy in the central government now."

China's two top leaders' view on the issue of Tibet and the role of His Holiness the Dalai Lama is widely divergent from the views held by the hardliner. During a visit to Laos at the end of March 2008, Chinese Premier Wen Jiabao told the international media, "Provided that the Dalai Lama renounces claims of independence, and in particular exerts his influence to stop the present violent activities in Tibet, and acknowledges that Taiwan and Tibet are inseparable parts of China, we can continue to resume dialogues with him."

President Hu Jintao in a call[57] to President Bush said, "If the Dalai Lama truly relinquishes independent Tibet claims, and stops splitting the motherland, and especially stops inciting and planning the violent and illegal actions in Tibet and acknowledges that Tibet and Taiwan are inseparable parts of China, we agree to continue dialogue with him."

During a visit to Japan later, Chinese President Hu Jintao said his government's attitude to the dialogue with the envoys of His Holiness the Dalai Lama was sincere. President Hu Jintao, as reported by Reuters on 7 May 2008, speaking after a summit with Japanese Prime Minister Yasuo Fukuda, said China's recent talks with representatives of Tibet's exiled Buddhist leader the Dalai Lama

---

[57] March 2008, before the Beijing Olympic.

had been "conscientious and serious" and said that the two sides had agreed to continue contacts.

Commenting on the attitude of these two leaders of China to the Tibet issue, Cao Xin, a political analyst, says, "The response of China's two topmost leaders reflects the reality that Tibetan Buddhism has powerful and perpetual influence on the Tibetan people, and it is also a reality that the Dalai Lama has profound influence on the Tibetan people as the religious leader of Tibetan Buddhism."

The writer says, "Based on the above-mentioned realities, some pragmatic policy changes should be considered. First, we need to distinguish between the majority of Tibetan religious believers and the government-labeled 'Dalai clique.' Given that the Dalai Lama is the only religious leader the Tibetan devotees recognize, religious faith and worship toward him cannot be handled simply as a typical political issue and should not be labeled as splitting the Motherland. This is in accordance with the policy of regional autonomy, and we must uphold it as the bottom-line."

The Question of the Splittist Flag:

On 31 March, 2008 Xinhua published a commentary by its writer, Cao Kai, entitled Dalai Lama a politician, not a simple monk. Apart from regurgitating the usual allegations, the writer says, "To make this government in exile status more credible, the Dalai Lama and his supporters produced a 'Tibetan national anthem' and 'Tibetan national flag', which had never existed before 1959."

The Chinese authorities call the Tibetan flag by various names. It is condemned as a "reactionary," "splittist" or "separatist" flag. It is sometimes called "the flag of the Tibetan government-in-exile." The Chinese state media also refer to it as the "Tibetan independence flag." Sometimes the Chinese authorities refer to it as the "snow lion flag."

One of the strange complaints of the Chinese authorities against the Tibetan exiles' use of the Tibetan flag, as implicit in these words of frustration and outrage, is that the Tibetan refugees had not sought permission from the Chinese authorities for the use of the motifs of the flag: the snow mountain and the snow lion. A report that appeared in China Daily on 11 April and reprinted in Xinhuanet.com the next day says this about the use of the snow mountain and snow lion. "They also used the image of our pure snow mountain and the just dauntless lion to make their so-called 'snow lion flag,' a cunning tactic to deceive kind-hearted people."

The Tibetan national flag is not an exile Tibetan invention. It has, in its various incarnations down the centuries, become a part of the Tibetan identity. The Tibetan flag with the snow mountain and the two snow lions existed long before communist China invaded Tibet. The origins of the Tibetan national flag go back to the time of King Songtsen Gampo in the 6th century. The various regiments of his army used different banners. One particular regiment, the Yu-ruTo, had a standard emblazoned with a pair of snow lions facing each other. Another regiment, the Ya-Ru Ma, had a battle standard with a single snow lion. The Tsang-Ru Lag regiment had an upright snow lion, leaping toward the sky. This tradition of having the snow lion in the banners and battle standards of the Tibetan army continued down the centuries till the Great 13th Dalai Lama standardized the present flag, which since then became the standard around which the Tibetan people rallied.

Since 2009, 142 Tibetans have self-immolated in Tibet.[58] 123 of them have died on the spot or shortly thereafter. The whereabouts and conditions of the surviving self-immolators remain unknown. All the self-immolators have called for "freedom in Tibet" and the "return of His Holiness the Dalai Lama to Tibet". However, instead of addressing the underlying grievances of Tibetans, the Chinese authorities have responded to these self-immolators with further repressive policies by heightening restrictions in Tibetan areas and dismissing the self-immolators as an "act of terrorism" and criminalize partners, friends and relatives of the self-immolators, as a preventive measure. In its annual report, released in April 2014, the US Commission on International Religious Freedom (USCIRF) confirmed this by stating that the self-immolation protests are directly released to Chinese efforts to control religious practice and culture of Tibetans, but Chinese authorities view these expressions of protest as criminal activities. In April 2013 officials in Dzoege, Ngaba Autonomous Prefecture, issued new rules extending criminal penalties to family members, fellow villagers, and monasteries of self-immolators.

The documents issued consists of 16 Articles- blacklisting family members of self-immolators, deprivation of political rights, deprivation of government employment, exclusion from all welfare benefits for three years, denial of ownerships of lands and houses, preventing from starting business, travelling embargo to Lhasa and foreign countries, deprivation of financial assistance and villagers, monks and nuns are subjected to 'legal education' campaign. There were more than 53 known cases of Tibetans who have been sentenced to varying prison terms from one to fifteen years under the alleged link with self-immolation protests. China's

---

[58] A report of UN, EU and Human Rights Desk, Department of Information and International relations, Central Tibetan Administration, Dharamshala. January 2016.

prosecutions of Tibetans in response to the self-immolation protests, which China thinks is a preventive measure to stop the self-immolation protest is actually, in a way compelling Tibetans to stage more tragic protests, including the self-immolation protests.

In a statement released on Tibetan self-immolation protests, Navi Pillay[59] urged the Chinese authorities to promptly address the longstanding grievances that have led Tibetans to take desperate form of self-immolation protest. She said that she was disturbed by "continuing allegations of violence against Tibetans seeking to exercise their fundamental human rights of freedom of expression, association and religion," and emphasized the "reports of detentions and disappearances, of excessive use of forces against peaceful demonstration, and curbs on cultural rights of Tibetans." She also urged China to consider 12 outstanding requests by various UN Special Rapporteurs and, to allow independent and impartial monitors to visit and assess the actual situations in Tibet. Various national, international communities and delegates expressed their concerns over rising self-immolation protests in Tibet.

Sino-Indian Relations Deepened, Military Ties Healthy:

China has presented an upbeat picture of its ties with India in a policy document on Asia-Pacific security, saying their partnership has "deepened", but skirted references to contentious issues like India's Nuclear Suppliers Group bid and efforts to get Jaish-e-Mohammed chief Masood Azhar banned by the United Nations

---

[59] Navi Pillay, the United Nations High Commissioner for Human Rights, 2, November 2012.

(UN). A white paper titled "China's Policies on Asia-Pacific Security Cooperation" said China and India made "new progress" in exchanges.

Chinese envoy proposes 'Treaty of Good Neighbourliness' with India. China's ambassador to India, Luo Zhaohui, has spelt out a four-step road map to implement a "long term vision for China-India relations", that would reduce tensions at a time when Beijing has reacted strongly to the Dalai Lama's recent visit to Arunachal Pradesh. Speaking in New Delhi, Luo recommended that Beijing and New Delhi "start negotiation on a China-India Treaty of Good Neighbourliness and Friendly Cooperation." He highlighted how well the 1993 Treaty for Peace and Tranquillity on the Sino-India Border had worked.

<u>Sino-India relationship: This is China's proposal to improve Indo-Pak ties:</u>

Amid increasing strain in Sino-India ties, China has proposed a four-point initiative to overcome differences and deepen relations which includes aligning its 'One Belt One Road' project with India's 'Act East Policy' and restart negotiations on a free trade pact. The proposal put forward by Chinese envoy Luo Zhaohui also includes starting negotiations on a 'China-India Treaty of Good Neighbourliness and Friendly Cooperation' and prioritising finding an early solution to the border dispute between the two countries.

"Firstly, start negotiation on a China-India Treaty of Good Neighbourliness and Friendly Cooperation. Secondly, restart negotiation of China-India Free Trade Agreement. Thirdly, strive for an early harvest on the border issue. Fourthly, actively explore the feasibility of aligning China's 'One Belt One Road Initiative' (OBOR) and India's Act East Policy," he said.

The Chinese envoy made the remarks while speaking at defence think-tank United Service Institution. Referring to Indo-Pak ties, Luo said China is willing to mediate to resolve differences between the two countries if both sides accept it. He said good ties between the two countries were conducive to regional stability and in China's interests. The development of China, India, Pakistan and the stability of the whole region call for a stable and friendly environment.

"Otherwise, how could we open up and develop? That's why we say, we are willing to mediate when India and Pakistan have problems. But the precondition is that both India and Pakistan accept it. We do this only out of goodwill. We do hope that there is no problem at all,"

Luo said.

"When the Mumbai terrorist Attack on November 26, 2008, took place, I was Chinese Ambassador to Pakistan, and I did a lot of mediation at that time,"

On the China Pakistan Economic Corridor (CPEC) which passes through Pakistan-occupied Kashmir, Luo said China has no intention to get involved in the sovereignty of and territorial disputes between India and Pakistan.

"China supports the solution of the disputes through bilateral negotiations between the two countries. The CPEC is for promoting economic cooperation and connectivity. It has no connections to or impact on sovereignty issues,"

"Even we can think about renaming the CPEC. China and India have had successful experience of delinking sovereignty disputes with bilateral relations before. In history, we have had close cooperation along the ancient Silk Road. Why shouldn't we support this kind of cooperation today? In a word, China is sincere in its intention to cooperate with India on the OBOR, as it is good for both of us,"

The Chinese envoy said the OBOR and regional connectivity could provide China and India with fresh opportunities, calling the project a major public product China has offered to the world.

"It is a strategic initiative aimed at promoting globalisation and economic integration,"

Referring to the views in India that China always puts Pakistan first when handling its relations with South Asian countries, he said the government always follows 'China first' policy and that "problems" are dealt with based on merit.

"I want to tell you this is not true. Simply put, we always put China first and we deal with problems based on their own merits. Take Kashmir issue for example, we supported the relevant UN resolutions before 1990s. Then we supported a settlement through bilateral negotiation in line with the Shimla Agreement. This is an example of China taking care of India's concern,"

On India's bid for the membership of the Nuclear Suppliers Group (NSG), he said,

"We do not oppose any country's membership, believing that a standard for admission should be agreed upon first."

The envoy's four-point suggestion to overcome differences comes at a time when the relationship between the two Asian powers has been going through a rough patch due to differences on a range of issues, including China blocking India's move to get Jaish-e-Mohammed (JeM) chief Masood Azhar banned by the UN and its opposition to India's bid for NSG membership.

On trade ties between the two countries, Luo said he was happy to see that China has contributed its share to India's development." Today, China is the second largest economy in the world, with a GDP of 11 trillion US dollars. China's development also benefited from India's participation. Luo said:

"We sincerely hope that India can become more developed, as it not only benefits Indian people but also creates more opportunities for China's development. Some people in the West misread China and tend to think that the 'Dragon' and the 'Elephant' are inevitable rivals, and that China would not like to see India developing. This conception is wrong. We hope to see India develop well and we are more than happy to help India develop to achieve common development."

On combating terrorism, he said China has been a victim of terrorism. "China strongly opposes terrorism; second, China is ready to work with India, Pakistan, Afghanistan and the international community in fighting terrorism, and believes that terrorism knows no borders; third, countries need to have compatible policies, consensus and actions in fighting terrorism."

Prospects for Future:

In the years 2002 and 2003, there was a glimmer of hope for dialogue between Tibetans and the Chinese government, when the latter hosted two visits by His Holiness the Dalai Lama's delegation. The first visit took place in September 2002. In the words of Lodi Gyari, leader of the delegation, his team had two missions-

a. To re-establish direct contact with the leadership in Beijing and to create a conducive atmosphere enabling direct face-to-face meetings on a regular basis in the future

b. To explain His Holiness the Dalai Lama's Middle Way Approach towards resolving the issue of Tibet.

On returning from the visit, Lodi Gyari said he had a positive impression of the attitude of leaders in Beijing. Then, in May-June 2003, Lodi Gyari and his team paid a second visit to Tibet and China. The visit came soon after a change in the leadership of the Chinese Communist Party and government. Lodi Gyari said he and his team had an opportunity to engage extensively with the new Chinese leaders and officials responsible for Tibetan affairs.

Later, the Chinese Premier Wen Jiaobao was quoted in the media as having said,

"So long as he (Dalai Lama) genuinely abandons his position on seeking Tibetan independence and publicly recognizes Tibet and Taiwan as inalienable parts of Chinese territory, then contacts and discussions between him and the central government can resume".

His Holiness the Dalai Lama has said for the umpteenth time that he is not seeking Tibet's independence. Moreover, China knows for certain that His Holiness' recognition of Taiwan as part of China is neither relevant to Sino-Tibetan dialogue, nor will it change the ground reality. China also knows that there is no moral justification for His Holiness to make such recognition.

<u>**Negotiation Strategy:**</u>

Those with any experience of negotiating with Beijing have found that it is a painful exercise, one that is fraught with frustrations and disappointments. Often, you will be led to believe that you are warming towards a solution, only to find the next moment that the carpet has been pulled from under your feet. But when you imagine that dialogue is no longer what they want, you will find yourself presented with a seemingly positive overture.

Where actually will this see-saw lead the Tibetan issue is anyone's guess. According to a Tibetan scholar at an Ivy League university in the United States, Beijing has long had a thoroughly prepared grand scheme for negotiating with Dharamsala. This scheme has three formats, namely the Hard-line, the Moderate, and the Liberal. As the contact proceeds, the Chinese leaders will swap back and forth between the three formats, depending on their perception of China's own strength, international situation, the strength of their "opponent", the internal power struggle within the Communist Party, and any number of other equations. This observation seems to hold true when one looks at the history of Tibet-China conflict, starting from the first peace initiative of His Holiness the Dalai Lama.

<u>**Heart and spirit of Tibet:**</u>

As the last delegates left Tibet, Beijing was re-thinking the wisdom of accepting the delegates. It took the Chinese authorities five more years before accepting the fourth delegation in July 1985. However, the six-member delegation was asked to confine its visit to the northeastern Amdo region. The logic was that the people of Amdo, having been liberated several years before other parts of Tibet, were more progressive in their outlook and thus less likely to feel any affinity to "the feudal lords of the past". Here also, the authorities had badly misjudged the popular mood.

Beijing was now left in no doubt that His Holiness the Dalai Lama was not really irrelevant to Tibet; rather, he was the spirit of Tibet, a rude shock to the power structure that derives sustenance from military might and a pervasive game of deception, played both within the Party rank-and-file and against the people under their rule, thanks to the lingering legacy of Mao, the Great Helmsman. However, it also meant that China has not since then accepted any Tibetan fact-finding mission into Tibet.

Further Initiatives for Dialogue:

In his turn, His Holiness continued to adhere to the belief that the problem of Tibet could be resolved through face-to-face meetings with the Chinese leadership. He was keenly aware that the past decades had created deep distrust and suspicion between Tibetans and Chinese, a chasm so deep that it would take huge efforts from both sides to inch towards the goal of reconciliation.

In September 1980 he offered to open a liaison office in Beijing to foster closer ties with the Chinese government and people. Then, on March 1981, he wrote to Deng Xiaoping and said:

> "The time has come to apply our common wisdom in a spirit of tolerance and broadmindedness to achieve genuine happiness for the Tibetan people" with renewed urgency. On my part, I remain committed to contribute to the welfare

of all human beings and, in particular, the poor and weak, to the best of my ability, without making any discrimination on the basis of nationality."

Hu Yaobang, China's Party Secretary (not to be mistaken for Hu Jintao), responded in July, proposing a "Five-point Policy toward the Dalai Lama". It asked His Holiness and members of the exile administration to return home, promising the Dalai Lama "the same political status and living conditions as before 1959". Members of the exile Administration were also promised jobs and living conditions that were "better than before". Conspicuous in this proposal was the absence of any reference to the core issue: the problems of Tibetans in Tibet. As far as His Holiness and the exile administration are concerned, their own status and "living conditions" are immaterial… a non-issue.

It was all too apparent that there should be greater efforts toward the exchange of views with Beijing. In April 1982 the Chinese government received a three-member delegation of the exile government for exploratory talks. The delegates asked for the reunification of all Tibetan areas "Kham, Amdo and U-Tsang" as a single political entity. Referring to Beijing's offer for Taiwan's unification with the PRC, the delegates suggested that Tibet deserved a greater degree of special status since its history, language, and culture were completely different from the Chinese.

Beijing responded by saying that the only basis for negotiations was the "Five-point Policy toward the Dalai Lama". It rejected the Tibetan demand by saying that unlike Taiwan and Hong Kong, Tibet had already been liberated and unified with China. The underlying message was clear: Since Tibet had no bargaining chips, there was no reason for Beijing to make it any concessions.

The overall situation in Tibet, though, was improving. Hu Yaobang's recognition of the special status of Tibet and the steps being undertaken to improve the situation on the plateau were seen as reassuring signs in Dharamsala. Earlier, in 1980, Hu had visited Tibet and announced sweeping policy changes to improve the living condition of the Tibetan people and to protect their culture. Hu had also proposed repatriation of 85 percent of Chinese officials and replacing them with Tibetans. If implemented, this would have been a significant step towards substantive autonomy for Tibetans.

Tibetans to this day remember Hu as a leader with courage and sincere desire to improve their lot. During His Holiness the Dalai Lama's meeting with the Chinese students at Harvard University in September 2003, he said he would perhaps have been in Tibet if Hu Yaobang had stayed longer in power.

Coming back to the 1980s, in February 1983 His Holiness told the Tibetan pilgrims in Bodh Gaya, in the Indian state of Bihar, that he wished to visit Tibet around 1985 if the situation continued to improve.

By then, the Chinese government had decided that it might not be a good idea to woo His Holiness back. In March-April 1984, China's Second Work Forum on Tibet recommended the transplantation of Chinese settlers into Tibet. It decided not to budge an inch from the "Five-point Policy Toward the Dalai Lama". A month later, Tibet Autonomous Region's Party boss Yin Fatang accused the Dalai Lama of treason and said Beijing would welcome him only if he admitted his "mistakes", a far cry from the early years of the post-Mao leadership when Gyalo Thondup was told that the Dalai Lama was not responsible for the March 1959 uprising in Lhasa.

Nevertheless, Beijing's multi-faceted diplomacy did accept another three-member delegation for exploratory talks in 1984. The delegates reiterated the demands made earlier in 1982 and voiced serious disquiet over the influx of Chinese settlers. They asked the Chinese leadership to accept His Holiness the Dalai Lama's proposal to visit Tibet in 1985.

China expressed reservations about the reunification of Tibet. It said no to the Tibetan demands, but asked the delegates to keep the proceedings confidential for a time being, reasoning that confidentiality was necessary to ensure the success of a negotiation as sensitive and complex as this.

When the delegates reached New Delhi, they were confronted by foreign correspondents, who asked for their reaction to Beijing's announcement that it had rejected their demand for Greater Tibet and a status akin to the one promised to Taiwan. As we have seen, the delegates had actually asked for a degree of autonomy that was greater than the one promised to Taiwan. They now realized that their interlocutors had acted in bad faith.

<u>Tibet seeks International Support:</u>

Signals emerging from the Chinese capital in the subsequent months were to reinforce the Tibetan suspicion that Beijing was only playing a game with them. Developments within the Chinese power structure also seemed to bode ill for Tibet. In 1987, Hu Yaobang was disgraced for his sympathy to Tibet and for being too soft on the Chinese student demonstrations of December 1986.

The only option now was to turn to the support of the international community, which incidentally had become more receptive to the cause of Tibet.

Deng Xiaoping's open-door policy had lifted the bamboo curtain to reveal that the egalitarian China of western intelligentsia's fantasy was nothing more than a totalitarianism of the new emperor, one whose pursuit of naked power and a place in the sunshine of history had sent millions to their death. Tourists and journalists who visited Tibet saw that China had enslaved, rather than liberated, the Tibetan people. Writers like Israel Epstein and Han Suyin had lied to the world. The intellectuals, who in their younger days had termed the Tibetan cause dead, were growing wiser. They now believed that Tibet was a cause that ought to live and triumph.

On 21 September 1987 His Holiness unveiled his Five-point Peace Plan for Tibet in his address to the US Congressional Human Rights Caucus. In this, he asked for:

1. Transformation of the whole of Tibet into a zone of peace.
2. Abandonment of China's population transfer policy.
3. Respect for the Tibetan people's fundamental human rights and democratic freedoms.
4. Restoration and protection of Tibet's natural environment and the abandonment of China's use of Tibet for the production of nuclear weapons and dumping of nuclear waste.
5. Commencement of earnest negotiations on the future status of Tibet and on relations between the Tibetan and Chinese peoples.

Beijing was outraged. Its propaganda mill worked overtime to demonize His Holiness the Dalai Lama. The demonology surrounding His Holiness grew by the hour, fanning the smouldering amber of Tibetan resentment. On 27 September 1987 the international media reported the first street demonstrations in Lhasa since the uprising of 1959.

Nine months later, His Holiness the Dalai Lama made public the formula for negotiations, which had been germinating since the 1970s when he discussed the concept of the Middle Way approach in a series of closed-door meetings with his cabinet in Dharamsala. Addressing members of the European Parliament in Strasbourg on 15 June 1988, His Holiness said he was willing to forego the idea of Tibet's independence in return for meaningful and substantive autonomy for a unified Tibet.

<u>Reactions to Strasbourg Proposal:</u>

The proposal came as a bombshell to the Tibetan public and the Chinese government alike. For the first time, there was no immediate reaction from Beijing. It was at a loss to decide as to how to respond to an initiative as revolutionary as that. On the other hand, the Tibetan Youth Congress, the largest non-governmental political organization of exile Tibetans, lost no time in expressing dismay. The youth president announced that no one had the right to give up the cause of Tibetan independence. This was the first time His Holiness' decision had triggered dissenting voices among the Tibetan community. Many Tibetans, despite their tremendous reverence for His Holiness, could not reconcile themselves to the notion of living with the country that had reneged on its own "17 Point Agreement"

On 23 June 2008, China's foreign ministry issued a vague press statement, saying its government would not accept "independence, semi-independence or disguised form of independence" for Tibet. Although the Strasbourg proposal was not named, the allusion was un-mistakable. China's suspicion was at play.

The exile Administration decided that there was a need to take immediate steps to allay Beijing's fears. On 27 July 2008 it issued a press statement, naming six members as its negotiating team. A Dutch international lawyer and two of His Holiness' overseas representatives were named as the team's assistants. Beijing's response came on 21 September, when its New Delhi Embassy contacted His Holiness' representative to express interest in direct talks with the Tibetan leader. On the following day, the Embassy issued a press statement, saying that the Dalai Lama could choose the date and venue for talks. "The talks may be held in Beijing, Hong Kong, or any of our embassies or consulates abroad. If the Dalai Lama finds it inconvenient to conduct talks at these places, he may choose any place he wishes." The Embassy, however, put three preconditions:

1. Beijing will not talk to the members of the exiled Tibetan administration.

2. No foreigner should be involved in the talks.

3. The Strasbourg Proposal cannot be the basis for talks, as it had not relinquished the idea of Tibet's independence.

While the exile Administration welcomed the offer of talks, it insisted that the Strasbourg Proposal was the only reasonable basis for talks. A statement issued from its headquarters in Dharamsala said, "Though we have different views and stands on many issues, we are prepared to discuss and resolve these through direct dialogue."

On 25 October Dharamsala informed the Chinese Embassy that it would like the talks to take place in January the following year in Geneva, citing the city's reputation as a neutral venue. Hours later, His Holiness' New Delhi Representative issued a press statement to this effect.

Meanwhile, China's United Front head Yang Minfu met Gyalo Thondup in Beijing and expressed strong displeasure with the exile Administration's action to publicize the venue and names of the delegates. He suggested that the talks should be held either in Beijing or in Hong Kong. Then, sounding a positive note, Yang added that although the 'Central Government' did not agree with some aspects of the Strasbourg Proposal, these could be discussed and resolved.

Two months later, the Panchen Lama passed away suddenly at his monastery, Tashilhunpo, in Tibet. On 7 February 1989 the head of the Chinese Buddhist Association invited His Holiness to attend a memorial ceremony for the Panchen Lama, due to take place in Beijing on 15 February. Years later, Beijing was to repeatedly fault His Holiness for turning down this most significant gesture of theirs. In this Beijing was not alone, for some international Tibet experts also maintain that His Holiness had lost an important opportunity there.

As far as Dharamsala was concerned, there was no way it could prepare for such a potentially momentous visit at such a short notice. Most of all, the Tibetan public opinion had to be prepared to prevent panic reaction. It does not take much imagination to realize that the Tibetan public would not readily agree to entrust the security of their "Wish-fulfilling Gem" to the communist government. As it was, there was widespread suspicion over the mysterious nature of the Panchen Lama's death, particularly when it came so soon after he announced publicly that Chinese rule in Tibet had brought more damage than benefit. Clearly, a longer time was needed to prepare for such a visit. One must not forget that the immediate cause of the 1959 uprising in Lhasa was the Chinese invitation to His Holiness to attend a theatrical performance at their military camp in Lhasa. Suspecting this to be a bait to abduct their leader, the populace of Lhasa formed a sea of human barricade around his palace. The Chinese crushed the uprising by pounding Lhasa with a rain of artillery shells.

In his turn, His Holiness offered to send a ten-member religious delegation to Tibet to offer prayers for the departed lama. China said there was no precedence for prayers on this scale and that it would not accept the delegation's two leaders as they were members of the Kashag (Tibetan cabinet).The exile Administration agreed to withdraw the two members and again contacted the Chinese government.

On 17 March the Chinese Embassy said its government would receive only two or three lamas as representatives of the Dalai Lama, but that they would be allowed to travel only to Tashilhunpo Monastery. In the same message, the Chinese government accused the exile Administration of having engineered the "troubles" in Lhasa and of having smuggled arms into Tibet. China was holding the exile Administration responsible for a series of protest demonstrations that followed the first one in September 1987. As a matter of fact, the demonstrations were spontaneous, and triggered as much by Beijing's anti-Dalai Lama Campaign as by disappointment at not seeing enough improvement in the situation in Tibet. It was equally hard to understand what "arms" Beijing was referring to. His Holiness had never called for violent action. Although a Chinese police station was burnet down, not a single shot was fired by the demonstrators. Neither was any weapon, apart from rocks and sticks, seen with them. The only gun they got hold of was the one they had snatched from a Chinese policeman, and this they smashed immediately on a rock.

Denying the allegations, the exile Administration challenged the Chinese government to produce evidence to back their claims. Against this background, the delegation did not get to visit Tibet.

Meanwhile, a quiet, but significant revolution was seeping through the lives of Chinese people. Religious faith was re-emerging to fill the spiritual vacuum left by the demise of faith in communist ideology. Many Chinese were turning to Buddhism, their traditional religion. The flow of information was freer now than ever before. Chinese scholars and intellectuals were beginning to appreciate His Holiness the Dalai Lama's Middle Way approach. At the same time, rampant corruption in the Communist Party establishment was creating a deep sense of disillusion among the people, who had expected Deng's "Get Rich" policy to benefit the common masses rather than the leadership and their cronies.

In June 1989 China was rocked by the Tiananmen Square demonstrations. The heavy-handedness with which the authorities crushed the demonstrations caused His Holiness deep dismay. Hundreds, perhaps thousands, of students and their supporters were killed. The tragedy ensured the ascendancy of Premier Li Peng's hardline faction. For the time being, there was a complete lull in Dharamsala-Beijing diplomacy.

Then in1991, His Holiness made an overture to assist in the search for the Panchen Lama's reincarnation. China rebuffed the offer by saying there was no need for "outside interference". A number of subsequent initiatives were cold-shouldered with outright disdain.

Among the exile populace there was now a growing feeling that the Chinese leadership was incapable of appreciating His Holiness' gestures, no matter how reasonable or conciliatory. Reflecting the popular mood, the Tibetan exile parliament passed a resolution on 23 January 1992, stipulating that the Administration should not initiate any move toward negotiation unless there was a positive change in the attitude of Beijing. However, in deference to His Holiness' on-going initiatives, the resolution stated that the parliament had no objection if overtures came from the Chinese side" either directly or through a third party.

This materialized three months later, when the Chinese Ambassador in New Delhi invited Gyalo Thondup to visit Beijing and explore possibilities for talks. The Ambassador said his government's position in the past had been conservative", but that it was willing to be "flexible" if the Tibetans were prepared to be "realistic".In Beijing, Thondup was treated to a list of accusations against the exiled leadership. There was no sign of the promised flexibility. Beijing's attitude had once again hardened between the time of Thondup's meeting with the Chinese Ambassador and his visit to Beijing.

In September 1992 China's State Council published the first ever White Paper on Tibet. Its Ownership and Human Rights Situation distorted historical facts to claim that China had owned Tibet for centuries. Lauding its own development in Tibet, the document portrayed traditional Tibet as the "darkest feudal serfdom" on earth. Such a confrontationist step did not bode well for the reconciliation process.

In that same month, His Holiness sent a personal memorandum to Deng Xiaoping and Jiang Zemin which asked Beijing to come up with its own proposal, since his proposal was not acceptable to them. He said, "If we Tibetans obtain our basic rights to our satisfaction, then we are not incapable of seeing the possible advantage of living with the Chinese." He also offered to dispatch a three-member delegation to explain his views. Beijing accepted only two members. In June 1993 the delegates discovered in Beijing that the leadership's hardline attitude had remained unchanged.

Deeply distressed, His Holiness advised a group of visitors from Tibet,"when you return home, tell the people to criticize me if the Chinese order them to do so. It won't change the reality. There is no point in you suffering on my account."

Then, in June 1998, American President Clinton took an initiative to revive the dialogue between His Holiness the Dalai Lama and China. In a joint press conference with President Jiang Zemin, Clinton asked the Chinese president to open dialogue with the Tibetan leader. Jiang replied,

> "As long as the Dalai Lama makes a public commitment that Tibet is an inalienable part of China and Taiwan a province of China, the door to dialogue and negotiation is open."

The Taiwan precondition surfaced for the first time.

The exiled Administration reacted immediately by saying that the issue of Taiwan's status was for the people of Taiwan and PRC to discuss and resolve.

Later, on 10 November 1998, His Holiness issued a press statement to say that he was seeking only meaningful and substantive autonomy for his people to preserve their distinct identity and way of life, and not independence or position for himself in the new dispensation. "With goodwill on both the sides, with a commitment to non-violence and reconciliation, we can work together to bring peace and stability to Tibet and lasting harmony between the Tibetan and Chinese peoples."

On the same day, the People's Daily of China carried a scathing front-page commentary, citing the Dalai Lama's act of publicizing the issue of Tibet as an indication of his insincerity. "The zigzagging on the issue of declaration indicates that the Dalai Lama has merely made tactical readjustments and played tricks, while his stance on Tibetan independence has remained unchanged in principle."

Before long, the exile Administration received reports of a secret meeting in China at which Beijing had made a decision neither to engage in serious talks with His Holiness the Dalai Lama, nor to secure his return to Tibet. This decision had been arrived at months before Clinton's visit. Addressing the third session of the Fifteenth Central Committee of the Chinese Communist Party on 14 January 1998, President Jiang Zemin reportedly said, "We have no need to engage in dialogues with the Dalai Lama. The issue of Tibet is about the ownership of Tibet, something that can't be discussed. The Dalai Lama's return to China will bring a great risk of instability. If he returns, we will not be able to control Tibet. The Dalai Lama is now fairly old. At the most, it will be ten years before he dies. When he dies, the issue of Tibet is resolved forever. Then, there will be no one to create problems for us. We, therefore, have to use skilful means to prevent his return."

The "skilful means" translates as feigning interest in dialogue for the benefit of the international public opinion, while making preconditions that would cut the ground under the feet of the Tibetans.

Today, as the exile Administration commits itself to making greater efforts than ever before to build a healthy atmosphere for dialogue and as it hopes that the current generation of Chinese leaders will see the folly of Jiang Zemin's waiting game, analysts have floated a number of speculations.

The first school of thought maintains that as long as China does not become a democracy, His Holiness' Strasbourg Proposal will not find acceptance there. They reason that while the Strasbourg Proposal is based on the liberal democratic principle, the Chinese communist system is based on the dictatorship of the Communist Party. Therefore, accepting the Strasbourg Proposal as a basis for dialogue would be seen as political suicide in Beijing.

Related to this is the argument advanced by a growing number of people who opine that the Communist leaders are actually nervous at the prospect of His Holiness' return. Having seen the tremendous reverence shown to His Holiness by the Chinese people in Taiwan, the Communist leaders' fear that they will become rallying point not only for the Tibetan people, but also for the Chinese Mainlanders.

Another school of thought believes that China's vacillating position on dialogue is only a mirror on the internal power struggle within the leadership. But it is only a matter of time before the liberal-minded leaders gain greater political clout. And when that happens, Beijing will, on its own initiative, reach out to His Holiness to find an answer to the problem of Tibet, they say.

The worry is that this may happen too late for both Tibet and China. His Holiness' Middle Way approach is as indispensable to China's long-term stability and unity, as it is to the socio-economic and cultural development of the Tibetan people. It is ill-advised for the Chinese leadership to assume that the Tibetan issue will die when His Holiness is no more. It is also wrong to assume that the issue of Tibet is about the personal status of the Dalai Lama. The Tibetan issue is about the rights, dignity and better quality of life for the Tibetan people. This aspiration will remain as long as there are Tibetan people. But rarely will history produce a leader, who puts the interests of peace and humanity above everything else. To wait for the passing away of such a leader is to squander the opportunity for lasting peace and harmony.

Tibet's human rights situation is deteriorating and requires urgent international intervention. The cycle of self-immolation in Tibet sends an unequivocal message about the need for China to re-assess its Tibet policy and to heed the aspirations of Tibetan people and their calls for freedom

The Central Tibetan Administration (CTA) based in Dharamshala, calls upon the China to immediately stop the ongoing, "patriotic re-education" and "strike hard" campaigns in monasteries and nunneries. Allow free and unrestricted access to Tibet by international media, observers, and UN mandate holders and respect the rights of Tibetans to live in dignity, and address their underlying grievances through dialogue-the only viable path towards a long-term sustainable solution to the current situation.

One of India's foremost security analysts and China experts, Jayadeva Ranade spoke to the staff of the Central Tibetan Administration on the topic, "The Prospect of Re-setting the India-China Relationship" at the Nyatri Hall on Wednesday , April 08, 2015.

Sikyong Dr Lobsang Sangay, who moderated the session, extolled Mr Ranade for his detailed and meticulous research work while acknowledging his contribution in keeping the fire for Tibet burning in the corridors of Delhi.

Mr Ranade began by giving a grand overview on the major changes that has shaped China following the Bo Xilai episode and the 18th Chinese Communist Party Congress in 2012 during which President Xi Jinping took over all three top posts in China.

He pointed out that the fall of the all-powerful former party chief of Chongqing, Bo Xilai, opened up the cracks in the Chinese system, proving that China's centres of power – the communist party, the People's Liberation Army and the vast security apparatus – were not as impervious to penetration as earlier thought. Following the debacle, Mr Ranade noted that there was a definitive hardening of stance within the core leadership of the Party, which in-effect led to the strengthening of the Party grip and the emergence of Xi Jinping as China's most powerful man since Mao Tsetung.

Mr Ranade observed that the coming to power of a reputedly decisive and bold Indian Prime Minister Narendra Modi, with a resounding mandate, and his policy of laying out geographic parametres with frequent visits to India's neighbouring countries has in fact fast tracked the resetting of India-China relationship.

Rubbishing earlier reports suggesting Xi's lack of control over the PLA during the intense military stand-off between India and China in the Chumar region of Ladakh, while Xi was on a State visit to India, Mr Ranade pointed out that all three concerned PLA commanders of the areas neighbouring Ladakh, Chumar and Depasang regions in Tibet were promoted to the rank of major general.

In response to a question, Mr Ranade stated that the present Chinese structure cannot continue for much longer as pressure resulting from the massive social and economic changes in China and the ongoing process of rectification within the PLA and the Party will force reforms.

Answering a question on the issue of Tibet, Mr Ranade took note of China's frustration over Tibet, which he said is becoming more and more evident with their continued failure in tackling issues such as the self-immolation protests. The former Additional Secretary in the Cabinet Secretariat assured the audience of the sympathy and support that Tibet enjoys among the Indian masses as well at various levels in the government. The talk was organised by the Tibet Policy Institute, a research centre of the Central Tibetan Administration.

The real intention behind the current ongoing urbanization in Tibet and its negative impact on Tibetan culture and identity and the Chinese government's policy of state territorialisation is through urbanization of Tibetan Plateau.

China's Belt and Road Initiative opportunity for India:

The Belt and Road Initiative (BRI) of China, which aims to link Asia with Europe for trade and other exchanges, represents an opportunity for India, former Foreign Secretary Shivshankar Menon said, "This does represent an opportunity for India. Even if some portion of what is proposed in the BRI is implemented, it will markedly change the economic and strategic landscape within which we operate," he said. Menon was speaking at a conference on 'The Belt and Road Initiative: India's perspectives on China's ambitious plan for infrastructural connectivity in Asia, Africa and Europe', organised by Mumbai-based Observer Research Foundation.

"The connectivity that BRI promises will benefit all the exporting countries in Asia which need to be better connected with their markets and suppliers. There are maritime and continental connectivity gaps in Eurasia which need to be filled,"

The Former National Security adviser said.

"There are evident advantages (of BRI) for the Chinese economy," he said, adding "BRI will set standards across countries and markets."

"If there is an attempt to exclude economic rivals or pursue political or security goals, the economic benefits will be limited,"

Menon said.

"There will be certain benefits for the Chinese economy and also advantages for the others who participate in the BRI,"

The former Foreign Secretary of India noted that not all projects under BRI were economically viable, suggesting that they would have some geostrategic motivations, for instance, the China-Pakistan economic corridor.

"It is very hard to see an economic justification for it. It is the strategic portion such as a port which has been implemented first,"

Menon said.

"For India, there is the added complication that it goes through Indian Territory under Pakistani occupation. Making a long-term investment on that basis seems to solidify and legitimise that occupation."

"Much of the planned BRI infrastructure is in regions and countries where security is weak and politics is unstable. Therefore, the risks to large-scale investments are considerable," he said.

Menon in his book on India's nuclear weapons doctrine, said, "China, like India, today is one of the most outspoken advocates of globalisation and multilateralism."

The BRI involves 65 countries and 4.4 billion people.

<u>**Suggestions for Dealing with the Tibetan Situation:**</u>[60]

1. At present the one-sided propaganda of the official Chinese media is having the effect of stirring up inter-ethnic animosity and aggravating an already tense situation. This is extremely detrimental to the long-term goal of safeguarding national unity. Such propaganda should be stopped.

2. The group of Chinese intellectuals support the Dalai Lama's appeal for peace, and hope that the ethnic conflict can be dealt with according to the principles of goodwill, peace, and non-violence. They condemn any violent act against innocent people; strongly urge the Chinese government to stop the violent suppression, and appeal to the Tibetan people likewise not to engage in violent activities.

3. The Chinese government claims that "there is sufficient evidence to prove this incident was organized, premeditated, and meticulously orchestrated by the Dalai clique." The Support Group hope that the government will show proof of this. In order to change the international community's negative view and distrustful attitude, we also suggest that the government invite the United Nation's Commission on Human Rights to carry out an independent investigation of the evidence, the course of the incident, the number of casualties, etc.

4. In their opinion, such Cultural-Revolution-like language as "the Dalai Lama is a jackal in Buddhist monks robes and an evil spirit with a human face and the heart of a beast" used by the Chinese Communist Party leadership in the Tibet Autonomous Region is of no help in easing the situation, nor is it beneficial to the Chinese government's image. As the Chinese government is committed to integrating

---

[60] The Sixth international conference of Tibet support groups Surajkund, Haryana, March 22, 2008, p.118-119.

itself into the international community, we maintain that it should display a style of governing that conforms to the standards of modern civilization.

5. The members of Support group note that on the very day when the violence erupted in Lhasa (March 14), the leaders of the Tibet Autonomous Region declared that "there is sufficient evidence to prove this incident was organized, premeditated, and meticulously orchestrated by the Dalai clique." This shows that the authorities in Tibet knew in advance that the riot would occur, yet did nothing effective to prevent the incident from happening or escalating. If there was a dereliction of duty, a serious investigation must be carried out to determine this and deal with it accordingly.

6. If in the end it cannot be proved that this was an organized, premeditated, and meticulously orchestrated event but was instead a "popular revolt" triggered by events, then the authorities should pursue those responsible for inciting the popular revolt and concocting false information to deceive the Central Government and the people; they should also seriously reflect on what can be learnet from this event so as to avoid taking the same course in the future.

7. They strongly demand that the authorities not subject every Tibetan to political investigation or revenge. The trials of those who have been arrested must be carried out according to judicial procedures that are open, just, and transparent so as to ensure that all parties are satisfied.

8. They urge the Chinese government to allow credible national and international media to go into Tibetan areas to conduct independent interviews and news reports. In our view, the current news blockade cannot gain credit with the Chinese people or the international community, and is harmful to the credibility of

the Chinese government. If the government grasps the true situation, it need not fear challenges.

9. They appeal to the Chinese people and overseas Chinese to be calm and tolerant, and to reflect deeply on what is happening. Adopting a posture of aggressive nationalism will only invite antipathy from the international community and harm China's international image.

10. The disturbances in Tibet in the 1980s were limited to Lhasa, whereas this time they have spread to too many Tibetan areas. This deterioration indicates that there are serious mistakes in the policies that have been adopted by Beijing with regard to Tibet. The relevant government departments must conscientiously reflect upon this matter, examine their failures, and fundamentally change the failed nationality policies.

11. In order to prevent similar incidents from happening in future, the government must abide by the freedom of religious belief and the freedom of speech explicitly enshrined in the Chinese Constitution, thereby allowing the Tibetan people to fully express their grievances and hopes, and permitting citizens of all nationalities freely to criticize and make suggestions regarding the government's nationality policies.

12. We hold that we must eliminate animosity and bring about national reconciliation, not continue to increase divisions between nationalities. A country that wishes to avoid the partition of its territory must first avoid divisions among its nationalities. Therefore, we appeal to the leaders of our country to hold direct dialogue with the Dalai Lama. We hope that the Chinese and Tibetan people will do away with the misunderstandings between them, develop their interactions with each

other, and achieve unity. Government departments' as much as popular organizations and religious figures should make great efforts toward this goal.

The past two decades have witnessed an unprecedented explosion of economic ties. In 1987, bilateral trade was a paltry US $117 Million; by 2011, it was over US $70 Billion. Both sides forecast that annual Sino-Indian trade will break the US $100 Billion mark in future. In the process, however, the trade surplus that India enjoyed in the early 1990s has become a US $27 Billion trade deficit. While China remains Pakistan's closest regional ally and the border dispute remains officially unresolved, Sino-Indian history since 1962 is essentially a history of non-violent, albeit often unfriendly, and coexistence.

Yet Tibet's future does not seem to be without a ray of hope. In fact, the Chinese leadership has shown its interest in having talks with the Dalai Lama's representatives. It means that there are still problems in Tibet beyond Chinese control. These problems, it appears cannot be wished away by continued military occupation or increasing diplomatic manoeuvres. A number of foreign visitors and fact-finding delegations of the Dalai Lama have shown that one of the fundamental problems still facing China in Tibet continues to be the obstinate but silent resentment of the Tibetan people against dominance. The clear indicators of this popular resentment began to emerge with the opening of Tibet to select foreign visitors.

There is virtual unanimity among strategic scholars in Asia and the West that the theatre for a Sino-Indian military rivalry is the Indian Ocean. India's naval build-up is a direct reply to the notion of a Chinese "string of pearls" a network of economically valuable ports and other assets. Yet the Indian tendency to see China's

Indian Ocean policy as one of military dominance rather than economic self-interest a view taken in light of the launch of China's first aircraft carrier in 2011 is excessive. It is symptomatic of a dichotomy that has been observed by, among others, Kishore Mahbubani, a veteran Singaporean diplomat and commentator on Asian affairs. Mahbubani notes that while in India, China is seen by the strategic establishment and the media as a virulent threat, Chinese coverage of India is much more positive. This is, of course, a reflection of the fact that China sees the United States, rather than India, as its equal; India is simply not its primary rival. Nevertheless, it is an observation that ought to give Indian policymakers pause.

The path of Sino-Indian relations is contingent on future economic and political developments within the two countries. Economic growth in India and China slowed in 2011. In the former, this was a consequence of policy paralysis; in the latter, it may be the beginnings of a longer-term change in growth trends. Even if Chinese growth slows to an annual rate of five percent, it would take India at least two decades to catch up with the size of the Chinese economy. Without sustained and rapid Indian economic growth, the relationship between China and India will not turn into a relationship of co-equals from the Chinese point of view. Political transition towards greater democracy in China could open up possibilities for much closer cooperation. India and China have both been guilty of abetting the suppression of democracy in Myanmar; if China embraces democracy, the onus will be on these countries, as regional powers, to promote democratic values throughout the region. Even on the most optimistic forecast, however, any such development is a decade away.

China and India have much to learn from each other, although sadly little learning takes place. India offers an example to China of the relatively peaceful integration of ethnic and religious minorities. Quite apart from China's economic growth, India should also attempt to match its successful regional diplomacy. Over the past few decades, India has squandered its in-built advantage as the leading power in South Asia by developing a reputation for high-minded arrogance. As a result, China has developed close ties with Nepal, Bangladesh, and Sri Lanka, countries within India's historic sphere of influence. Without much fanfare, China has also embarked on a serious-minded program of developing sustainable sources of energy, something to which India has given insufficient attention.

China's heightened rhetoric over Arunachal Pradesh and its closeness to Pakistan, when juxtaposed with anti-Chinese sentiment in India, suggest a gloomy prognosis for future ties. China is the only permanent member of the UN Security Council to refuse to support India's bid for a permanent seat on that body. But the relatively peaceful reality of the disputed border and burgeoning trade between the two countries suggest that India and China have a much greater need to cooperate than they acknowledge. A close friendship, *Hindi-Chini Bhai Bhai* redux, is certainly not in the cards. But the two countries can, and ought to, aspire to much better than an Asian version of the Cold War, or even the peaceful, yet uneasy coexistence of the 1970s and 80s. A true global "pivot" to Asia, and the accompanying claims of an Asian Century, is much more plausible if Asia's two largest countries see the productive potential of more mature and responsible ties.

<u>**Peaceful Settlement of Tibet:**</u>

Yet one hopes for a peaceful political settlement in Tibet. The future of Tibet concerns not only the Tibetans themselves; it touches the nerve centre of strategic interests of several neighbouring countries. Although China objects as a matter of principle to any third party mediation in Sino-Tibetan negotiations, yet the Chinese leaders must realize how complicated and inter-connected the Tibetan question is. The Dalai Lama has insistently demanded the withdrawal of people's liberation Army troops from Tibet, and China is quite correct in that there cannot be any unilateral withdrawal of Chinese troops without corresponding withdrawal of Indian troops from the Indian Himalayas.

It is a fact that with the fall of Tibet there has been a silent arms race between India and China. From both sides there has been a progressive diversion of insufficient resources, which could be used to feed the poor peasants, to arms building. Neither the withdrawal of Chinese troops from Tibet nor for that matter any progress in the Sino-Tibetan dialogue can be expected without an overall improvement in Sino-Indian relations. Once the Sino-Indian relations get improve, one can hope that India will not short-sightedly and naively capitalise on a Hindi-Chini bhai-bhai trip, as it did in the 1950s; but that it will try to work towards a peaceful political settlement in Tibet. Events since 1962 have shown that the moral selling of Tibet to China cannot solve India's security problems, which are a function of geo-politics closely inter-connected with Tibet. One cannot wish away geography; it is there. Simultaneously, China kept in view the India's legitimate interest in Tibet as it directly affects Indian national security, just like China. Mr. Muchukund Dubey, former foreign secretary of India and president of the Council for Social Development, a New Delhi-based research group, said

"We need to handle the matter delicately,"

"That delicacy involves abiding by very specific rules about what Tibetans can do in India, despite India's democratic roots. Tibetans have every right to organize themselves, but they cannot indulge in political activities,"

Mr. Dubey said.

"The Tibetan man's self-immolation was certainly political, he said, as well as "embarrassing" to the government of India."

China's economy is almost three times as large. They are typically regarded as the greatest economic and political threat to Western dominance in the decades to come. It is thus surprising, and unfortunate, that so little of this burgeoning China-India literature deals with the relationship between the two countries. After all, the potential rivalry between China and India could be the defining international issue of our times. Justifiably dubbed "the contest of the century" by The Economist in 2010, this remarkably complex relationship is often poorly understood, sometimes even within the two countries.

In July of 2010, India's foreign secretary, Nirupma Rao, met with the Dalai Lama at his residence. The substance of their discussions was not disclosed, but they happened a week after India's national security adviser, Shiv Shankar Menon, met officials in Beijing to talk about, among other things.

<u>Question of Doklam</u>:

Doklam is a narrow plateau lying in the tri-junction region of Bhutan, China and India. Doklam is situated roughly 15 KM. southeast of the Nathu La pass that separates India and China. On the western edge of the Doklam plateau is Doka La, which connects Sikkim with Tibet (Chinese Government Claim) or linking Sikkim to western Bhutan (Bhutanese and Indian government Claim)

Chinese army attempted to extend a road from yadong to south of the Doklam plateau. But according to Bhutanese government, China attempted to extend a road that previously terminated at Doka La towards the Bhutan Army camp at Zompelri. According to New friendship treaty (Signed between India and Bhutan) it is mandatory for Bhutan to take India's guidance on foreign policy with border sovereignty and not require Bhutan to obtain India's permission over arms imports.

Recently PLA construction party entered the Doklam area and attempted to construct a road. It is our understanding that a Royal Bhutan Army patrol attempted to dissuade them from this unilateral activity. The Ambassador of the Royal Government of Bhutan (RGOB) has publicly stated that it lodged a protest with the Chinese Government.

The Bhutan Foreign Ministry also issued a statement underlining that the construction of the road inside Bhutanese territory is a direct violation of the 1988 and 1998 agreements between Bhutan and China and affects the process of demarcating the boundary between these two countries. In keeping with their tradition of maintaining close consultation on matters of mutual interest, RGOB and India have been in continuous contact through the unfolding of these developments.

India is deeply concerned at the recent Chinese actions and has conveyed to the Chinese Government that such construction would represent a significant change of status quo with serious security implications for India.

In this context, the Indian side has underlined that the two Governments had in 2012 reached agreement that the tri-junction boundary points between India, China and third countries will be finalized in consultation with the concerned countries. Any attempt, therefore, to unilaterally determine tri-junction points is in violation of this understanding. Where the boundary in the Sikkim sector is concerned, India and China had reached an understanding also in 2012 reconfirming their mutual agreement on the "basis of the alignment". Further discussions regarding finalization of the boundary have been taking place under the Special Representatives framework.

India cherishes peace and tranquillity in the India-China border areas. It has not come easily. Both sides have worked hard to establish institutional framework to discuss all issues to ensure peace and tranquillity in the India-China border areas. India is committed to working with China to find peaceful resolution of all issues in the border areas through dialogue.

CHAPTER V
CONCLUSION

With a written history of more than 2000 years, Tibet had remained an independent, sovereign State. However, The People's Republic of China (PRC) justifies its occupation of Tibet by claiming that Tibet has been part of China for around 800 years. However, China's claim is not supported by facts. Tibet has cultivated and maintained a unique culture, written and spoken language, religion and political system for centuries, making its historical territory the world's 10th largest nation. Tibetans are a uniquely distinct race, different from all the surrounding peoples. It's time for a comprehensive, open dialogue between India and China to promote communication and connectivity in diverse spheres and preserve the peace on our shared borders.

The Chinese Ambassador to India, Luo Zhaohui, recently put forward some suggestions for improvement of bilateral ties between China and India. What did Mr. Luo say? The remarks were obviously prepared as the Chinese do not speak off-the-cuff in public spaces. He suggested a 'friendship and cooperation treaty' and a free trade agreement (FTA) to boost bilateral relations and joining of hands on China's One Belt, One Road (OBOR) initiative, and added that the time is ripe for both countries to reap some 'early harvest' outcomes (based on negotiations held so far) on the unresolved boundary question.

The Ambassador chose to make these remarks at the newly-established Ji Xianlin Centre for India-China Studies at the University of Mumbai campus lent some symbolism to the occasion. Ji Xianlin was one of China's foremost modern

Indologists and a protagonist of friendship and civilisational understanding between India and China.

Could the Ambassador's statement be part of an effort within the Chinese establishment to review relations with neighbours like India, given the strategic uncertainties generated by the advent of Donald Trump's administration in the U.S. and his unabashed negativity towards China? Mr. Trump's phone call with the Taiwanese President, Tsai Ing-wen, before he took office; his proclaimed intention to impose punitive tariffs on Chinese goods; and the new U.S. Secretary of State, Rex Tillerson's thinly disguised threats against China's building of artificial islands in the disputed areas in the South Sea have all generated concern in Beijing.

It is not known whether these ideas articulated in Mumbai by the Chinese envoy have been discussed at the government-to-government level previously. It is possible that some of them, particularly the 'early harvest' concept relating to the boundary, may have been broached in some form or other by the Chinese side. Sectors of the boundary, like Sikkim and the middle sector (Uttarakhand/Himachal Pradesh), are by and large free of the disputes that one sees in the western (Jammu and Kashmir) and eastern (Arunachal Pradesh) sectors. But 'solutions' that segment the border instead of ensuring an overall comprehensive settlement of the boundary may be difficult to accept, especially for India.

A treaty of friendship and cooperation between the two countries recalls the 1954 "Panchsheela" Agreement which essentially tied up the status of Tibet but also outlined the Five Principles of Peaceful Coexistence principles that became empty words over the ensuing years as the relationship slid into conflict and then took years to revive. The 1993 and 1996 agreements on peace and tranquility and confidence-building in the India-China border areas reiterated the five principles and also spoke of the non-use of force and the concept of mutual and equal security. While India need not spurn the latest Chinese overture made by Mr. Luo, and would do well to explore what the proposal entails, the devil is always in the detail.

As for trade and economic relations, Mr. Luo's idea of an FTA is no doubt forward-looking. Trade between India and China has grown to an annual volume of $70 billion (2015-16). India has made a strong pitch for Chinese investments under Make in India in infrastructure development, solar energy and smart cities. Recent reports, however, also suggest security hurdles faced by Chinese firms seeking to invest in India. An FTA that is goods-centred will obviously not benefit India given the huge trade in goods imbalance that favours China. An FTA that is comprehensive, covering goods and services, cross-border investment, R&D, standards and dispute resolution would be worth exploring. As some Indian scholars have observed, "An FTA with China may have benefits that escape quantification and transcend economics."

Connectivity build the sinews of successful diplomacy today. The rigor of borders and sovereignties has triumphed over any consensus-building on connectivity and cooperation beyond borders. India's own reaction to China's OBOR has been hedging and tentative, mainly because of the CPEC through Pakistan-occupied Kashmir. At the same time, India is a part of the frontline membership of the Asian Infrastructure Investment Bank(AIIB) that is bolstering OBOR.

The Chinese have today chosen to disregard the sovereignty issues surrounding the dispute between India and Pakistan over the State of J&K, despite the provisions of the 1963 China-Pakistan Boundary Agreement which conceded the disputed nature of the territory (in what Pakistan now calls Gilgit-Baltistan but what India claims as part of Jammu and Kashmir) covered under the agreement. This is a crucial reason for India's reservations about OBOR. The Chinese are seen by India to have acted in disregard of Indian sensitivities on this matter, which is a cause for legitimate concern. The questions however is, whether despite this, India should as a test of the Chinese approach, and with reference to OBOR, explore the development of connectivity between Tibet and India, especially through the Sikkim sector into Bengal. The old route between Lhasa and Kolkata via Nathu La was the most easily traversed route and may still be, despite the road networks constructed by the Chinese in Tibet between Tibet and mainland China, via land and sea, up until the mid-20th century. This is a road that provided for the transport of goods and services between Tibet and the outside world through India.The case for its revival requires a serious examination and should not be dismissed cursorily. Nathu La is already the crossing point for border trade between India and the Tibet Autonomous Region. A true indicator of Chinese positivity would also be approval for India to open a Trade Office in Lhasa in place of the old Consulate General that operated there until 1962.

An opening of ties between India and the Xinjiang region of China is also worth examining. Providing for air connectivity between Urumqi, the capital of Xinjiang province, and New Delhi as one of the OBOR linkages, for instance, would help the promotion of people-to-people ties and trade and commercial contact and could also help open a new chapter in counter-terrorism cooperation between India and China. The two countries have a common interest in curbing religious radicalism and terrorism. Kashmir and Xinjiang, both contiguous neighbours, have similar challenges posed by terrorism and separatist movements.

India-China relations can definitely do with some new thinking and new ideas, and from that point of view, the Chinese Ambassador has done well to articulate his outlook, however modest, on how more bilateral cooperation can be promoted. The long peace between the two countries, stretching from the 1970s to the present day, deserves preservation and not disturbance. It is entirely in the self-interest of each country to ensure this.

Competitive coexistence, with a clear delineation of areas of difference and how to manage them, the promotion of business and people-centred connectivity, and mutual confidence-building with tension-reduction measures cannot do any harm. The border problem, by virtue of its complexity and size, will take its time to resolve.

Maturity of approach, and strategic patience while each country is preoccupied with the demands of internal and external equilibrium and balancing, offers a constructive way forward. The modus Vivendi of the last few decades are easily disturbed as recent events have shown. China as the larger neighbour must take the initiative to ensure that trend is halted.

Its approach on NSG, Masood Azhar, and other terrorist activities in PoK, to name a few, has cast long shadows on the relationship. China cannot expect India not to pursue her legitimate interests in ensuring the security of its periphery, and to promote ties with countries like the U.S. and Japan and ASEAN partners in the Indo-Asia Pacific. All these countries have extensively evolved and developed relationships with China. Likewise, our cooperation with them need not hinder a productive, comprehensive, open and frank dialogue between India and China that is aimed at preserving and promoting good contact, communication and connectivity in diverse spheres as also the peace on our shared borders of the last few decades.

Tibet is very important to China's sense of nationhood, says CFR's China expert Adam Segal. "There is a fear that if Tibet gets independence, Uighurs and Taiwan will want independence." Segal notes that Chinese authorities have frequently suggested that they are just waiting for the Dalai Lama to die, expecting Tibetan nationalism to disappear after his death, but says this may be a miscalculation. "I think the more radical Tibetans would direct the movement for independence after Dalai Lama's death."

Experts agree that unless there is political reform within China, the resolution of the Tibetan question remains bleak. "The historical question was never unsolvable," says Barnett. "It would not have been a problem necessarily if China had been able to develop policies for Tibet that were acceptable to most Tibetans." In November 2008, the Dalai Lama said his efforts to bring autonomy to Tibet had failed so far and called for a meeting of Tibetans from around the world to consider the future of the Tibetan movement. The meeting, which took place on Nov. 17-22 in Dharamsala, India, drew more than five hundred Tibetans. Though the meeting closed with what was described as a "strong endorsement" of the Dalai Lama's "middle-way" approach, participants also "clearly stated" they might seek independence if talks with China do not bring progress "in the near future."

The March 2008 anti-government clashes in Tibet and other regions in China brought the decades-long dispute once more into the international spotlight demonstrating the depth of historical disagreement over the territory. Tensions between China and Tibet have persisted since People's Republic of China was founded in 1949. China says Tibet has been a part of China for many centuries now, a claim refuted by many Tibetans. Chinese authorities use this claim to support their sovereignty over the territory while proponents of the Tibetan independence point to periods in Tibetan history when it enjoyed self-rule. Meanwhile, Chinese government policies in Tibet have fed the conflict. These include restrictions on cultural and religious freedoms of Tibetans, attempts to change the demographics of the region through migration of ethnic Chinese, and unwillingness to open dialogue with Tibet's exiled spiritual leader, the Dalai Lama. Experts believe the dispute over Tibet will persist as long as China refuses to speak to the Dalai Lama, who has been in exile in neighbouring India since 1959. China, however, has sought to bypass the 73-year-old Dalai Lama and concentrated instead on efforts to control the process that will determine his successor.

When the Dalai Lama sought exile in Dharamsala in northern India in 1959, India arguably became a key player in the conflict. India now is home to about 120,000 Tibetans, the world's largest Tibetan community outside Tibet. But since 1952, India has always regarded Tibet as an integral part of China and does not encourage overt criticism of China by Tibetans in exile. Sumit Ganguly, a professor of political science at Indiana University, is openly critical of the Indian policy. "If India is indeed a liberal democracy," he says, "it must be willing to speak out about the gross Chinese human rights violations."

Ganguly believes India's administration can exert pressure on China by allowing Indian Tibetans to demonstrate peacefully without interference, and by treating the Dalai Lama as a head of state instead of a spiritual leader. But there are many Indian analysts who believe otherwise. "There is interest on both sides, very deep interest, to see that what is happening is not allowed to upset the apple cart—the present momentum of India-China relations," says Mira Sinha Bhattacharjea, former director of the Institute of Chinese Studies in New Delhi. Relations between India and China, long fraught with resentments including a short border war in 1962, recently have warmed. China became India's biggest trading partner in 2007. The two countries have also seen a thaw in diplomatic relations.

Challenges:

The border dispute remains, particularly in the short-term, a primary source of friction. While it is not an "active" dispute in a military sense, it regularly manifests itself in the course of Sino-Indian relations. In 2009, for instance, China was incensed by the Asian Development Bank's decision to grant funds to a project specifically allocated to "Arunachal Pradesh." China was able to exercise its diplomatic muscle successfully: the Bank was forced to remove all references to Arunachal Pradesh. For several decades, China's rhetoric on Arunachal had been relatively muted, but it has been ramped up considerably since 2006. Current Chinese policy is to claim all of Arunachal as part of China. The Indian response has been to increase troop presence in Arunachal, as well as the larger neighbouring state of Assam. Yet the Indian military build-up is dwarfed by the 400,000 People's Liberation Army (PLA) troops near the Sino-Indian border.

While the more hawkish elements in the Indian strategic community see all this as a cause for alarm, the Indian military establishment offers a more sober analysis. While the incidences of Chinese "intrusion," accidental or otherwise, have steadily increased, the vast majority of these have been minor and caused by confusion over the exact Line of Actual Control. It is simply inaccurate to state that China and India have an ongoing "hot" border conflict. Nonetheless, China's inflamed rhetoric ought to be taken seriously. It is impossible to rule out small-scale clashes over the border in the future, although the idea that Arunachal will trigger another full-scale war is far from plausible.

The end of the Cold War and the long-term peace between China and India did not deter Sino-Pakistani relations from improving as well. China and Pakistan see each other as a bulwark against India. China has long since replaced the United States as Pakistan's largest military supplier, as well as its only supplier of nuclear technology in the post-AQ Khan era. In October 2011, India registered with Beijing its objection to the presence of at least 3,000 PLA troops in Azad Kashmir, the territory claimed by India, but administered by Pakistan since its seizure in the Indo-Pakistani war of 1948. China's decision to station PLA troops in an area central to the Kashmir dispute is a clear evidence of an abandonment of any pretense of neutrality on the issue. This has clear potential to impede the betterment of Sino-Indian relations in the future.

While the rapid expansion of bilateral trade is by far the most positive long-term development in relations between China and India, even economic ties can be a source of tension. Much of the illegal mining in the southern Indian states of Karnataka and Andhra Pradesh, which is responsible for environmental degradation and massive instances of political corruption in the region, was linked to the growing Chinese demand for iron ore, which was being smuggled to China. Most recently, a business dispute between Indian traders and locals in the Chinese city of Yiwu led to the alleged kidnapping and torture of Indians, who were accused of reneging on agreements.

Finally, the continued presence of the Tibetan government-in-exile in the Indian mountain city of Dharamshala is a permanent cause of Chinese frustration, albeit one that is rather peripheral to the relationship as a whole.

However, as Ranjit Kalha pointed out in *India-China Boundary Issues: Quest for Settlement* (2014), in 2007, confronted with the enhancement of the Indo-US strategic relationship, the Chinese baulked and its foreign minister Yang Jiechi blandly told his Indian counterpart that "the mere presence of populated areas [in Arunachal] would not affect Chinese claims on the boundary". This was followed by other measures such as the denial of a visa to an IAS officer of Arunachal Pradesh, issuing stapled visas for visitors from Jammu and Kashmir and stepping up its patrolling of the Line of Actual Control, especially in the areas where the Indian and Chinese perceptions of the line overlapped. Simultaneously, it also enhanced its nuclear ties with Pakistan to counter the Indo-US nuclear deal. Kalha believes that "the Chinese had decided to utilize the unsettled border as a part of coercive diplomacy to put 'pressure' on India".

Given the long and complicated history of Sino-Indian border negotiations, multiple possibilities flow from Dai's interview and his specific reference to Tawang. It could well be simply the personal views of a retired senior official. On the other hand by bringing the issue of China's claim on Tawang into the Indian public domain it could be a calculated move aimed at putting India on the defensive. Finally, it could actually presage a move back to give life to the 2005 political parameters agreement. China is currently under a great deal of pressure from internal as well as external developments. Historically these are the moments in which it becomes more amenable to settle its disputes.

There are some hints in that direction in another report of Dai's interview which notes that China did not see India as a rival and neither did it seek to contain it. Not only was China "delighted" with the evolution of India's relations with other countries, including the US, Dai went out of his way to laud India's "independent foreign policy" based on its pursuit of "strategic autonomy."

Interestingly, the Dai interview coincides with the Sino-Indian spat over the planned visit of the Dalai Lama to Tawang later this year, his first since 2009. A Chinese spokesman has said that China was "gravely concerned" over the development and that it would "bring serious damage to peace and stability of the border region and China-India relations." In his remarks, the spokesman accused the "Dalai group" of putting on "dishonourable acts in the past on the boundary question." It is not exactly clear what he meant by that.

Tawang may well have emerged as the focus of Sino-Indian relations, which revolve around the fulcrum of Tibet. Tawang is the most important monastery of Tibetan Buddhism outside Tibet. It was the birthplace of the fifth Dalai Lama and was established at his behest in 1680-81. What the Chinese worry about it that it may be the place where the current Dalai Lama, who is 81, decides to reincarnate. Even though they insist that only they can certify a Dalai Lama, it could well lead to an invidious position from their point of view.

India has long recognised that Tibet is a part of China, but their insecurities there have been fuelled by their own shoddy and, in the past, brutal, handling of their minorities. The more recent Chinese mishandling of their relations with India has resulted in New Delhi refusing since 2010 to reiterate in joint statements that Tibet is part of China. The current Indian government, which invited the Prime Minister

Tibetan of the government-in-exile for the auth taking ceremony of Prime Minister Narendra Modi, has hardened the Indian position. In December 2016, President Pranab Mukherji became the first president in decades to welcome the Dalai Lama in the Rashtrapati Bhavan, albeit on the occasion of a function organised by the Kailash Satyarthi Foundation.

At the end of the day, given India's categorical acceptance of Chinese sovereignty over Tibet, Beijing needs to accept that New Delhi has important equities in Tibet. These are not just born out of the history of Tibetan Buddhism or geography, but the fact that Tibet has been an important neighbour of India and our historical, cultural and economic interaction has been going on since antiquity.

A New Opportunity for India:

India must seize the opportunity that has opened up today to review and recalibrate its policy on Tibet. The decision of the Dalai Lama to abdicate his political responsibilities and hand them over to a democratically elected 'Kalon Tripa' is a momentous development in the history of Tibet. It reflects the profound wisdom and foresight of the Dalai Lama. Felicitations are due to the new Kalon Tripa, Dr. Lobsang Sangay. I have followed his articles, speeches and interviews with great interest and admiration. It is also fortunate that the Tibetans today have in addition to their supreme spiritual guide, the Dalai Lama, two young leaders from the next generation: the 17th Karmapa and the Kalon Tripa, Dr. Lobsang Sangay. There are few suggestions for the action India needs to take as a part of a bold new policy on Tibet.

1. Removal of restrictions on the activities and movements of the Dalai Lama and the Karmapa. All directives in place must be withdrawn which require political leaders and senior officials not to be seen in public with the Dalai Lama and the Karmapa. It is an affront to India's sovereignty that such restrictions are in force to accommodate the wishes of another country. The Dalai Lama and the Karmapa deserve our deepest respect as internationally acclaimed spiritual leaders. There should also be an end to the suspicions and reservations that a section of our establishment has against the Dalai Lama and the Karmapa. There were powerful voices in the Indian establishment in the 1950s and 1960s that the Dalai Lama should be sent back to Tibet. There are segments of our establishment today that are keen to accord the same treatment to the Karmapa.

2. India must identify completely with efforts to preserve Tibetan culture and Tibetan Buddhism. When Buddhism was virtually wiped out from India, the land of its origin, the Tibetans undertook to nurture this rich heritage over the centuries. The time has come for India to reciprocate this gesture. There is a hope that the Dalai Lama can be persuaded to take the leadership in bringing the scattered schools of Buddhism in India under a common umbrella.

3. It is time to remove the refugee tag from the Tibetans who have opted to make India their home. Those who are inclined to be Indian citizens must be granted citizenship without going through harassing procedures. Tibetans must be given the same privileges as the citizens

of Nepal and Bhutan. Young Tibetans of Indian origin should be encouraged to form Indo-Tibet friendship societies or associations which will promote the awareness of Tibet among the Indian public.

4. Reciprocity must be the guiding principle hereafter in India's response to Chinese demands on the status of Tibet.

5. India must not hesitate to express concern over the violation of the human, cultural and religious rights of the Tibetan people, not only in the Tibetan Autonomous Region, but in other states with significant Tibetan population. This should not be seen as a challenge to China's sovereignty but as a part of India's continuing advocacy of the rights of vulnerable communities across the world.

6. India must publicly and vehemently oppose the construction of dams on the Brahmaputra / Yarlang Tsangpo which would divert its waters away from India and Bangladesh. This should be taken up by India both bilaterally and at appropriate global forums.

India must be equally firmly in expressing concern over the ecological damage caused by the unrestricted development projects in Tibet. It is the source of ten major rivers and numerous glaciers which provide sustenance to two million people in Asia.

BIBLIOGRAPHY

BOOKS

Ardley, Jane. Tibetan Independence Movement: Political, Religious and Gandhian Perspectives, Routledge Curzon, London, 2002.

Bell, Sir Charles. A Unique Figure in World History, 'Portrait of the Dalai Lama' London, 1946.

Bishop, Isabella L. Among the Tibetans, Asian Educational, New Delhi.

Chand, Attar. Tibet: Past and Present: A Select Bibliography with Chronology of Historical Events 1660-1981, Sterling Publishers, New Delhi, 1982.

Chattopadhyay, Alka (tr.) Tibetan Chronological Tables, Certral Institute of Higher Tibetan Studies (Dalai Lama Tibeto- Indological Series), Varansi.

Chopra, P.N. Social, Cultural and Political History of Tibet, Criterion Publication, New Delhi, 1989.

Claude, Arpi, Dharamsala and Beijing, Lancer Publishers, LLC, ePub.

Dash, Vaidya Bhagwan. Tibetan Medicine with special reference to Yoga Sataka Indo-Tibetan Relationship, Library of Tibetan Works and Archives, Dharamshala, 1980.

Dharmananda, Subhuti. FROM TIBET TO INDIA: History of the Attempted Destruction of Tibetan Culture in Tibet and the Efforts at Preservation of Tibetan Culture in Exile.

Fergusson, W.N. Land and People of Tibet and China: In the early twentieth century, Sharda Prakashan, Delhi.

Gallagher, Belinda. Encyclopedia of History from the origins of humans to the modern day, Miles Kelly publishing Ltd. UK, 2015.

Gosh, Suchitra. Tibet in Sino-Indian Relations 1899-1914, Sterling Publishers Pvt. Ltd., New Delhi

Grenard, J. Tibet: The Country and Its Inhabitants, Cosmos Publicasions, Delhi, 1974.

Ham, Peter Van. Indian Tibet Tibetan India, the Cultural Legacy of the Western Himalayas, Niyogi Books, New Delhi, 2015.

Harrer H, Return to Tibet, 1984 Butler and Tanner Ltd., London.

Holdich, Thomas. Tibet, the Mysterious, Inter India Publications, New Delhi, 1983.

Hutheerging, Raja (ed.), Tibet Fight for Freedom, Bombay, Orient Longmans, 1960.

Jackson, David P. and Jackson Janice, A. Tibetan Thangka Paitings: Methods and Materials, Seridia, London

Jha, Hari Bansh. Tibetans In Nepal, Book Faith India, 1992.

Karnick, V B. China Invades India: The Story of invasion Against the background of Chinese History and Sino Indian Relations, 'Sino-Indian Relations' Allied Pub. Bombay,1963.

Kashyap, Dr. Subhash C. The Political Philosophy of Dalai Lama selected speechs and writings, 'Sino- Tibetan Relations', Rupa Publications New Delhi, 2014.

Kerr B, Sky Burial: An Eyewitness Account of China's Brutal Crackdown in Tibet, 1993 Noble Press, Chicago, IL.

Kolmas, Josef. Tibetan Books and Newspapers (Chinese Collection), OttoHarrassowitz -Wiebaden, 1978.

Krull, Germaine. Tibetans in India: A case study of Mundgod Tibetans, Allied Publishers, Bombay, 1968.

Lahiri, Latika. (tr.) Chinese Monks in India, Motilal Banarsidas, Delhi, 1986.

Ligetti, Lonis. (ed.) Tibetan and Buddhist Studies Commemorating the Zooth (in 2 vols), Anniversary of the Birth of Alexander, Akademiai Kiado, Budapest, 1984.

Madan, P.L. Tibet: Saga of Indian Explorers', 1864-1894, Manohar, New Delhi.

Mckay, Alex. Tibet and the British Raj The Frontier Cadre 1904-1947, Library of Tibetan Works and Archives, Dharamshala, 2009.

Mckey, Alex. (ed.) History of Tibet (in 3 Vols), Routledge Curzon, London, 2003.

Mehrotra, L.L. India's Tibet Policy an Appraisal and Options, Tibetan Parliamentary and Policy Research Centre New Delhi, 1997.

Nadwi, Dr. Abu Bakr Amir-uddin. Tibet and Tibetan Muslims (Translated from urdu By Prof. Parmananda Sharma), Library of Tibetan Works and Archives, Dharamshala, 2004.

Petech, L. China and Tibet in the Early 18th Century: E. J. Brill, 1972.

Richardson, H.E. Tibet and Its History, Oxford University Press, London, 1962.

Samten Jampa and Tsyrempilov Nikolay. From Tibet Confidentially, Secret correspondanc of the Thirteenth Dalai Lama to Agvan Dorzhiev 1911- 1925, Library of Tibetan Works and Archives, Dharamshala, 2012.

Sankrityayan, Rahul. My Third Expedition To Tibet (1936) Tr. By Sonam Gyatso, Library of Tibetan Works and Archives, Dharamshala, 2012.

Sergius L. Kuzmin. Hidden Tibet, History of Independence and Occupation (Edited by Andrey Terentyev Translated from Russian by Dmitry Bennett), Narthang, St. Petersburg, 2010.

Shah, Girraj. Tibet, the Himalayan Region: Religion, Society and Politics, Kalpaz Publications, Delhi, 2000.

Sinha, Nirmal Chandra. Tibet: Considerations on Inner Asian History, Firma K.L. Mukhopadhyay Calcutta, 1967.

Sperling, Elliot. The Tibet-China Conflict: History and Polemics, East-West Center, Washington DC, 2004.

Stein, R.A. Tibetan Civilization, Faber and Faber, London.

Thapa, Deb Bahadur. Tibet Past and Present (in 3 vols) Kalinga Publications, Delhi, 2003.

Tsering Shakya, The Dragon in the Land of the Snows: A History of Modern Tibet Since 1947, 1999 Columbia Press, New York.

Tsering, Lhasang. India's Tibet: A Case for Policy Review.

Tucci, Giuseppe. Tibet: Land of Snow, Oxford and IBH Publishing, Calcutta, 1973.

Wangdue, Gyaltse Namgyal. Political and Military History of Tibet Vol. I (Tr. By Yeshi Dhondup) Library of Tibetan Works and Archives, Dharamshala, 2012.

Welley, M.S. Through Unknown Tibet, Asian Educational Service, New Delhi.

<u>REPORTS AND BULLETIN</u>

IDSA Task Force Report, Tibet and India's Security: Himalayan Region, Refugees and Sino-Indian Relations, Institute for Defence Studies and Analyses, New Delhi May 2012.

Norbu, Prof Dawa T. Sino Indian Ties, *Ranzen* Summer, Vol. 19, 1994.

Hongyu, Wang, Sino-Indian Relations: Present and Future *Asian Survey* Vol. 35, No. 6 Jun, 1995. University of California Press.

ABOUT THE AUTHOR

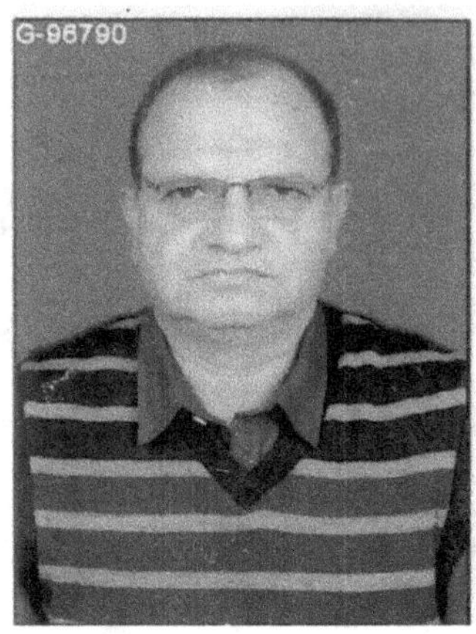

Dr. Bhuwneswer Kumar Tyagi is Professor and Head, Department of History, Jawaharlal Nehru Smriti Govt. PG College, Shujalpur, Madhya Pradesh, India. Dr. Tyagi has done his M. Phil from Meerut University, Meerut, India and he was awarded Ph. D. in History by Vikram University, Ujjain for his doctoral thesis entitled "India's Trade Relations with Central Asia". He has attended many national seminars and History Congresses. He has also published research papers in national journals. He has completed two Minor Research Projects awarded by the University Grants Commission, India on 'Relations of India and Central Asia and its future Prospects' and 'Indo -Tibetan Relations'. He has also co-edited three bi-lingual books published by the college viz., *Bharat Mein Vaishvikaran Evam Udarikaran: Prakriti evam Prabhav* (2012), *Aadhunik Bharat Nirman: Saamajik, Aarthik evam Rajnitik Paryavaran* (2014) and *Mahila Sashaktikaran: Chunautiya evam Sambhavnaye* (2019). He specializes in Ancient Indian History and International Relations.